The Green Bell

Paula Keogh

16pt

9781525243165

Read How You Want
LARGE PRINT BOOKS, BRAILLE & DAISY

Copyright Page from the Original Book

AFFIRM press

Published by Affirm Press in 2017
28 Thistlethwaite Street, South Melbourne, VIC 3205
www.affirmpress.com.au

*All reasonable effort has been made to attribute copyright and credit.
Any new information supplied will be included in subsequent editions.
All reasonable effort has been made to verify the assertions in this book. Events, locales and conversations are recounted to the best of the author's recollections.*

Epigraph and quotes from the poems of Michael Dransfield taken from *Michael Dransfield: Collected Poems,* UQP, 1987, edited by Rodney Hall ('Geography III', 'The inspector of tides', 'Minstrel', 'Portrait of the artist as an old man', 'The hermit of green light', 'Miss Havisham', 'Chaconne for a solipsist' and 'Like this for years' also appear in *Michael Dransfield: A Retrospective,* UQP, 2002, selected by John Kinsella) are used with kind permission of University of Queensland Press. Other quotes from Michael Dransfield's poems, letters and diary entries used with kind permission of the Estate of Michael Dransfield.
'The Man Watching' [3 I. excerpt] from *SELECTED POEMS OF RAINER MARIA RILKE, A TRANSLATION FROM THE GERMAN AND COMMENTARY* by ROBERT BLY. Copyright (c) 1981 by Robert Bly. Reprinted by permission of HarperCollins Publishers.
Lines on p.231 from 'Five Days Old' by Francis Webb (*Collected Poems*, edited by Toby Davidson) used with kind permission of UWA Publishing.
Lines on p.208 and 227 from 'Little Gidding, Four Quartets' and lines on p.15 from 'The Hollow Men' by T.S. Eliot (*Collected Poems 1909–1962*) used with kind permission of Faber and Faber Ltd.

National Library of Australia Cataloguing-in-Publication entry available for this title.
Title: The Green Bell / Paula Keogh, author.
ISBN: 9781925475524 (paperback)

Main cover image: Christopher Ash
Background cover image: Shutterstock/Voyagerix
Author photo by Roslyn Osborne

TABLE OF CONTENTS

Paula Keogh has a PhD in creative writing from La Trobe University and received the 2015 Affirm Press Mentorship Award for the development of *The Green Bell* at Varuna, the National Writers House. She taught at RMIT for nine years, and has lived in Canberra, Adelaide and Toronto, but considers Melbourne home.

For my daughter,
Rowan Kathleen Mangan,
with love

In writing this memoir, I have relied on my personal notebooks and letters, Michael Dransfield's poems and journals, his letters to me, my medical records, and conversations with members of my family.

In the process of remembering, I discovered that memories draw on both reality and imagination to recreate the dramas that make up what remains of our past. They are the subjective traces of our lived experience, and I am constantly amazed by their generative power, their capacity to bring people to life, and the gifts of identity and meaning that they give us.

In the interests of privacy, I have changed the names and physical characteristics of certain people in this story, including the medical staff and patients at the Canberra Hospital.

GEOGRAPHY III

in the forest, in unexplored
valleys of the sky, are chapels of pure
vision. there even the desolation of space cannot
sorrow you or imprison. i dream of the lucidity of
the vacuum,
orders of saints consisting of parts of a rainbow,
identities of wild things/of
what the stars are saying to each other, up there
above the concrete and minimal existences, above
idols and wars and caring. tomorrow
we shall go there, you and your music and the
wind and i, leaving from very strange
stations of the cross, leaving from
high windows and from release,
from clearings
in the forest, the uncharted
uplands of the spirit.

–MICHAEL DRANSFIELD

October 1972

For an hour or so, the night has no secrets. We've slipped out of the hospital and are walking along a path by the lakeshore. Above us, the full moon shines on a quicksilver world – so bright and dark and so in awe of itself, I want to kneel down and pray.

I breathe in the smell of eucalyptus and feel the chill in the air. I'm free and as light as a bird. At the edge of the lake I step along the top of a stone wall, one foot in front of the other, my arms spread like wings to keep my balance. Michael walks on the path beside me, talking about comets and solar winds, and I glide in his dream of space, feeling vast, wide open to the night. A wind blowing through me.

I tell him I no longer have a name. 'Names close you off from the world.'

He laughs, and I can tell he knows exactly what I mean. 'You've become a nymph,' he says. Then he spins around on one leg in a spontaneous dance, hair frizzing out from under his beanie, his coat unfastened and loose. With his vintage air force boots strapped below the knee, he looks like a wild man from the Russian steppes, a rangy Cossack. He whirls around again, this time catching me in his arms, and we are dancing, lake and trees flashing by, his eyes bright as onyx.

Inside my head, a voice breaks through from another place. 'The night doth magnify my soul,' it says, and I think of angels. Someone or something has reached inside me and turned up the volume of my being, so loud all I hear is wings and silence.

'Catch me if you can,' Michael calls, disappearing into a spinney of trees. I follow but I can't find him. When I call out his name, he replies from above, and I look up into a gum tree silhouetted against the sky. At first I can't make out where he is, and then I see him lying on a branch sloping upwards from the trunk. His arms are outstretched, his body suspended in the moonlight above me.

My eyes lock on the image.

I see a castaway in an oversized coat and heavy boots extended on a cross, facing the sky. Where his shirt has ridden up, his skin is white and exposed, and his unbuttoned coat hangs below the branch like a broken sail.

When Michael slides down from the tree, I put my arms around him. Darkness has shown its other face and I want to protect him. But inside his coat he's as thin as a bone, and all of a sudden I can't stop shivering.

1

M Ward, September 1972

The day room is where I wait – for time to pass, for something to happen, for meaning to return. Windows along one of the walls allow light to enter, but the space seems grey as if a faint dusting of ash hangs in the air and covers the surfaces. Patients hunch over tables or rest deep in the lounge chairs beside the walls, staring into the distance or mumbling to themselves. Occasionally someone erupts: a fist comes down on a table, or a chair is knocked to the floor. I'm startled for a minute, then the gloom settles over us again like the memory of a death.

My usual place is a lounge chair in the corner. My legs jerk back and forth, and my arms are folded tightly around my chest. Other patients are also sitting alone, settled in after the morning medication ritual, resigned to wait out the long stretch of time until the bell is rung and lunch is served. I'm hyper-alert, aware that everything around me is thick with meaning. The curtains, the tables, the pictures on the wall – they all mean something sinister, something I can't quite grasp. I write poems in my notebook but I can't speak to others of the noise inside my head. When they call me 'Paula', I tell them that I'm Julianne, but they don't hear me. I say it louder. They turn away.

I stare at a print of a Sidney Nolan painting that hangs on the wall opposite the windows. It shows Ned Kelly inside a heavy suit of black armour riding a horse across the desert towards the horizon. His back is turned to the viewer, and he is alone in the landscape. Blue and white sky shines through an oblong in his helmet. I stare at him, willing myself into his armour, longing for my head to fill with the colour blue, with space. I want to be Ned, turn my back on this life and ride a horse across the desert to the horizon. Ride out of this room into the distance.

I try to keep away from other patients. If someone comes close I pick up my pouch of tobacco and, with the concentration of a watchmaker, I roll myself a cigarette. To be in close proximity with another person is excruciating; their energy is too strong, too intrusive. The occasional exception is a patient I think of as 'the Man from Kosciuszko'. A bear of a man, he sometimes talks to me of his work on rescue missions in the Snowy Mountains. I like him because he has a dog, a border collie called Jessie. One night he broke down in tears and told me how much he missed her.

Sometimes I have visitors who join me in the day room – my parents or friends who sit awkwardly, talking in low voices. Conversations tend to drift into delicate silences until someone thinks of an item from the evening news or a piece of family gossip. An effort is required by us all in the giving and the taking. Someone will start speaking but lose confidence, leaving words dangling in the air. Eruptions of laughter sound like bursts of scripted applause. My world is inaccessible to anyone attempting to enter, to engage. I'm always tired after visitors leave. Sad and tired.

When my mother comes in, she brings a small bunch of sweet peas or lavender from her garden. She always asks, 'How are you today, love?' I turn away. How can I reply? The question 'How are you?' is complicated. I can't look at her. It's me that's not right. Not my kidneys or my tonsils. My self. How can it reply? It has lost the language of the everyday, the gestures and rituals of relationships. I sometimes think that my words are germs, infecting anyone who hears them.

***

One Friday afternoon, two weeks before I'm taken to the psychiatric ward of the Canberra Hospital, I ride my bike to the National Library to find journal articles for an essay on the Russian Revolution. Perhaps there are signs that I will soon have a breakdown, but I don't read them, don't realise what they mean. I've been under pressure with deadlines, but I don't for a moment see that M Ward is my future.

Once inside the library I pause in the entrance hall, taking in the light that streams through the high leadlight windows. I look up and hear music – orchestral music playing in the red, yellow and purple patterns of glass, a kaleidoscope of sound. I turn around, elated. When I look away to see if other people have heard it, the music stops. Confused, I come back to myself and walk into the reading room.

Later, as I'm leaving the library, a young woman appears, sailing towards me, sandy hair flowing behind her. Her height and stride are familiar, and when she speaks I remember her from 1968, four years ago, my first year at university. The year my friend Julianne Gilroy died. The woman in front of me was in the same philosophy tutorial as Julianne and me, studying the work of Descartes and arguing points about truth and doubt. Now, as we talk, I realise that former classmates have not forgotten my dramatic departure from university at the end of that year.

'Is everything okay now?' she asks, appraising me.

'I'm fine,' I say with a bright smile. 'Absolutely fine.'

Once down the library steps, I take off on my bike, riding hard. I'm frustrated that no matter how hard I try to pass for normal, I simply can't get away from my past. Not for the first time, I imagine myself escaping Canberra and making a new start somewhere, a warm place where no one knows me.

On impulse, I decide to take the long way home, across Kings Avenue Bridge and around the lake. With the winter air slicing my cheeks and the wind in my hair, I turn onto the long arc of the bridge and begin to cross the pale waters of Lake Burley Griffin.

Canberra has no past and it feels beautiful but empty, like a Zen garden – although the scale is wrong. It seems to have originated in a dream of intersecting circles and radiating lines too vast for human reach and footstep: a sculpted city of lonely monuments, architectural curiosities and glassed-in government buildings spread out around the artificial lake like pieces of an abandoned board game. Too new to have settled into the earth, too geometrical to have emerged from it, the city has a lightness of being, a cool detachment. It doesn't yet belong to the landscape. It's the image of a future without a history.

Canberra's inhabitants have no past here either, no stories that connect them to this place. A cluster of federal public service employees, they were sent from Sydney and Melbourne to administer government departments and populate the capital. Uprooted and separated from their extended families, and surrounded by distance and absence, they burrowed into suburbs and learned to love their cars.

My family was part of this interstate migration; we left Sydney when I was nine years old to start a new life here. The trees that now provide a canopy were only saplings in my childhood. Streets were laid down through paddocks, houses appeared, and suburbs spread across the valley. I grew up playing in partially constructed buildings, watching the Molonglo River rise across the flood plain and create Lake Burley Griffin. Waiting for the future to arrive in a place where everyone came from somewhere else and no one was old.

I ride around the lake, past the windswept fountain, past Blundells Cottage and the rotunda, racing towards Black Mountain, the Brindabella Ranges in the distance. I imagine Canberra as an immense gallery through which I glide, observing and admiring. Steel and concrete join the architecture of earth, sky and water to create a city of grand statements and wide streets, swept clean by the wind from the Snowy Mountains. In the icy afternoon sunlight, it shines like a mirage. Depth is illusory. A vision of sky drifting in the lake. The haunting sound of carillon bells echoing across the water.

My city, myself. Floating above my body, the city floating above the landscape, I'm as light as light. I remember myself as a young girl, twirling around in my floral skirt, my rope petticoat brushing my thighs, my arms spread wide. Barely aware of flesh and blood, and hardly knowing I was of the earth, I lived in air and sunshine. I banished darkness from my conscious world and ignored my body's secrets, the guilty blood, the night terrors. In the country's empty capital I grew up taut and shiny. Being good, being pure, being happy. Nice.

***

The evening after my visit to the library, I ride my bike to my waitressing shift at Dimitri's restaurant and stay on for an after-work party. The restaurant is tucked away in the ground floor of a 1960s motel on Northbourne Avenue, and it has the feel of a hideaway. With its dim lighting, low ceiling, and brown and beige decor, it looks like any other motel dining room – but its appearance is deceptive. For Dimitri's family and friends, it's the village *taverna* they left behind on the other side of the world. On occasional Saturday nights, once the customers have left and our work is done, the records are brought out, the stereo is turned on, and the party begins.

Dimitri's family and friends arrive in a flurry of greetings, claiming tables and carrying plates dripping with baklava and lemon cake. I don't speak Greek but tonight I feel I do. Eating *mezethes* with the others and drinking wine, I'm sure I know what people are saying. Listening to their voices, I see dark interiors and sense unspoken longings. I hear the playful teasing of old friends, the flourishes of gossip. When they break into English to include me, I take on the rhythms and inflections of their speech, enjoying the shapes the words make in my mouth.

In odd moments, I seem to be watching myself as I gesture expansively – flicking my long hair back from my face and flouncing my skirt around my knees. My mind is straying, playing with me, like the aura some people experience before a migraine. I drink water and try to steady myself.

From across the table, I watch Dimitri smoking a cigarette in his customary extravagant way, talking and laughing – a short man with a wide smile and a voice that comes from deep inside his chest. You can hear his breathy conversation from the other end of the restaurant, even when he's speaking softly. He treats all his workers as if they are part of his extended family – and, in fact, most of them are. Everyone is included in his after-work parties.

When the music starts to play, I feel a rush of anticipation. This is my favourite time of the night. I push my chair back and make my way to the dance floor with the others, swaying to the beat. 'Wait for me,' says the effusive Cosima, laughing as she follows. 'You've become such a Greek. A green-eyed Greek.'

As usual, I stumble at first, feet in my way. But then the music lifts me up and around, and soon I'm dancing with the others, moving to the faster rhythm, raising my hands high. In a single movement, I step forward with the women, creating an inner circle while the men in the outer circle surround us. As one, they move forward, eyes wild and dark, approaching with a surge of masculine energy.

Something shifts, and I discover a reciprocal power in myself. Sensations are magnified. I turn with the women to face the men, and I've never before felt so strong, so fierce. I stamp my foot down, and again I raise my hands high. My body wakes to a faster pulse as the dancing becomes wilder. Shadows loom on the periphery of my eyes and chandeliers flicker like jewels. I'm in ecstasy, a whirling dervish but with more abandon, more release, and a kind of grace I've never felt before. As if my body has its own kind of wisdom, an energy that knows exactly each movement, each step, each turn.

Fireworks explode in my mind; colours thrill me. The bouzoukis play through my soul, vibrate through my body, pound in my blood. I'm possessed by the music and the dance; by a power, primal and sensual.

I lose myself. Raising my hands high, stamping my foot down.

When the music stops, I'm dizzy, blinking fast, the room circling around me. I find my way back to the tables with the others. They're also breathing hard. Their eyes shine like marbles. I'm disoriented. Elated. Not sure what just happened.

***

The days pass, but I'm still under the spell of the dance. I've been winging my way from tutorial to lecture to coffee with friends. Now, in a quiet moment, I stand at the window of my room at Ursula College watching a sunset light up the sky like a visual anthem.

I sense something coming, something big, but I don't know what it is. Lights are brighter, moods are wilder, and thoughts race across my mind. The world has become stranger and more exciting than I ever imagined it could be. And I want this strangeness, this excitement. It's as if I'm in a canoe speeding along a river, feeling the rushing wind, hearing thunder moving closer, too exhilarated to care that Niagara Falls is around the bend.

At moments I sense that something isn't quite right, but it's impossible to satisfy this appetite, this restless craving for more and more life. I'm not simply happy – I'm euphoric. I'm doing mental cartwheels; my body is singing.

I no longer care about the essays I should be writing. The point is to live, not waste time trying to understand this philosophy, that ideology, this theory. Kierkegaard, Marx, Skinner. I've spent months working through my books, staying up late trying to make sense of them. But now all I want to know is, what did their authors feel, how did they live? There's nothing in the textbooks on that, so I've packed them away under my bed.

In my narrow room, I dance to the soundtrack of *Zorba the Greek* and study the map of Greece pinned to my noticeboard, circling the names of places I just have to go to. I see myself living on a Greek island, swimming in the 'wine-dark sea' and learning the language. I stay up all night sitting on my bed, smoking cigarettes and reading Sappho's poetry. I try to write poems that have the sensual immediacy of hers – fragmentary, impressionistic pieces – but I can't stem the streams of writing that flow from my pen.

One night, in a sustained burst of energy, I read *Prospero's Cell* by Lawrence Durrell. I'm excited by his descriptions of the bohemian lifestyle of 1930s Corfu, and I can't wait to live there. I decide to buy a ticket to Athens as soon as I have the money, whether or not I've finished my exams. I'm thrilled by the idea of myself in sunglasses and a wide-brimmed hat, sitting at an outdoor restaurant on Samos or strolling along the black-pebbled beach on the volcanic island of Santorini. Or maybe I'll work on a fishing boat off the coast of Ithaca.

In my room crowded with anti-war posters and an overflowing bookshelf, I'm seized by the power I experienced while dancing at Dimitri's. I want to live like that: connected, open, passionate.

I spin like a top across the surface of my days, unable to resist the energy driving me forward, unable to sleep. Sitting at a desk in my favourite corner of the library, I read Joseph Conrad's *Heart of Darkness* and make copious notes, heart pounding at the thought of 'the horror, the horror'. In an English tutorial, feeling reckless and inspired, I share with the other students the ideas racing through my mind. As I speak, I'm there, deep in the African night.

It's not like me to be so vocal; I'm usually the quiet student who's done the week's reading but lacks the confidence to speak.

Growing up, I was serious and obedient. I tried to be one of the good girls, stay safe, play by the rules. But too much has happened over the past few years, and I no longer believe in that. Goodness doesn't protect you from loss, from friends dying, from confusion and madness. I no longer care if I break the rules. Earnestness clings to me, though, however hard I try to shed it. Even when I rebel, I go about it in a considered way, more an intellectual position than an inspired act of mutiny.

'You know you'll go to hell,' my mother said when I told her during my first year at university that I'd lost my faith and would not be going to Mass. I was sorry she was suffering on my behalf, but her warning has never bothered me. I no longer believe in the fires of that particular hell.

I believe in this life, and I want to throw myself into whatever it offers. I'm determined to have adventures, travel the world, discover truer ways of being. In the past, I looked up from my books, saw the wilder side of campus life and longed to be part of it. Now, my inhibitions are dissolving. I can dance. I can speak.

***

One evening, a blind is pulled down on this bright world.

On a television set in the college lounge room, I watch a broadcast on the Munich massacre. The world is reduced to a black-and-white screen. The images are graphic, shocking. I'm catapulted back into a world of terror, into the inner turmoil caused by the political and social conflicts of the past ten years – particularly the Vietnam War. I feel I can't take one more explosion of violence, one more senseless death.

Later, in my room, I sing along with Bob Dylan until I'm numb from the density of emotion in the songs. In the morning I play and replay 'Farewell Angelina', looking out at the wintry landscape of the campus, the black lace of tree branches, the sodden lawns. Sitting at my desk, I fill a notebook with pages of poetry, stopping only to press my hands against my eyes for the relief it gives. I read Walt Whitman's poems and, inspired by his advice, 'Dismiss whatever insults your own soul', I throw out my collection of articles and leaflets on the war. I draw a yellow butterfly and tape it to the wall above my desk.

While my inner world is full of poetry and imaginings, the world outside feels distant and empty. I want to take hold of something with both hands, something external to myself, and make it matter to me. But I've been unable to reach through to anything solid.

I miss my friend Julianne. She was the one person who really knew me. After she died, I felt on the outside of life. I was standing in the darkness, looking through a window into a room glowing with light and love. I could see the fire blazing in the grate, and people sitting around a table, talking, eating and laughing. But I was locked out.

On the night I danced at Dimitri's, I became one of the people in that room, at that table. I'm now, inexplicably, on the inside of life. But the energy that's rushing into me is immense, irresistible, a waterfall, a torrent of sounds and colours, thoughts and sensations that sweeps me up, swirls me around, draws me under. I'm freefalling into the whirlpool at the bottom of Niagara.

***

I wake late in the day, late for my class. I take the quickest route across the campus, rushing along the track to the creek, across the footbridge and between the rows of white poplars, heading towards the building that houses the English department. I run up the stairs and open the door into a room crammed full of students and as stuffy as the under-deck of an old trawler. The tutor lifts his head and glances at me as I take a seat. He murmurs something and looks back at his book. I'm sure he's just been talking about me.

He clears his throat and begins reading aloud T.S. Eliot's long poem 'The Hollow Men'. His voice drones through the airless room, dirge-like and despairing, conjuring images of formless shapes, shadows, rats in dank cellars. His voice is like quicksand. I'm drawn down into it, and I can't get traction. It's dense and sonorous, and it's suffocating me. I'm in 'death's dream kingdom', and nothing is as it was. I hold on to the sides of my chair. I'm falling.

I hear a *crack* inside my head – not loud, but long. A splitting sound.

The tutor's voice is breathy and elongated as if resonating through a pipe. My head is a radio; sounds are coming from inside it, not from the world around me. I look down at my hands and try to steady myself. The voice proclaims: 'The eyes are not here/There are no eyes here/In this valley of dying stars'.

I grasp with absolute certainty the only real thing: I'm alone and freezing cold.

I'm dying.

When the reading ends, silence descends over me like a hood. I have to get back to my room as quickly as possible. I must not talk to anyone. *In this valley of dying stars.*

***

It's been night for a long time. I've put an extra blanket on my bed, and I'm wearing a jumper over my pyjamas but I can't get warm. I'm so cold I can't move. The college is asleep; the only sound I hear is the distant humming of the central heating system.

It's clear that, like Julianne, I've died.

As though I was awake one moment and asleep the next, I have no memory of the transition. But it happened. All life has left me. Even my room is lifeless, the ghost of a room, with my bedside lamp throwing shadows on the walls and moonlight reflecting in the mirror like the pearly sheen of an abalone shell.

Being dead feels real to me. It feels right. I've crossed the river, and I know who I am. I've come home. *I'm dead. I'm Julianne.* With her eyes I see the bookcase and the desk as if for the first time. I see how forthright the angles are, how precise the junctures, how smooth the flat planes of the wood. And these hands in front of my eyes are her hands. My hands. I'm free at last of the hollow world, the meaningless gestures. This death is true. *I know who I am.*

But as the night wears on, I fall into another kind of death. It's no longer a relief to be dead – it's terrifying. Thoughts attack me, a tirade of accusations and profanities that see betrayal in the things around me. The books on the shelves are full of lies, my coat on the back of the door will never keep me warm, and the drawing of a yellow butterfly has no meaning. I see the world now as the dead see it.

There are no eyes here.

In the morning, I try to wash my face in the bathroom sink, but I can't make sense of the water spiralling down the plughole into darkness. All is sinister, uncanny. I see death in everything, as if it has always been there but I haven't noticed it before. I'm seeing with Julianne's eyes now, and information is crashing in from all directions.

At breakfast in the college dining room, I line up along the buffet counter. The mouth of the woman behind the trays of food is making sounds in a language I don't recognise. I take some cereal and find a chair at an empty table. As I eat, I realise that the thoughts in my head are being broadcast from a distant site. I feel a bit sick. I'm sure war has been declared. Something terrible is about to happen. Across the room, people's eyes are communicating in code; everyone's blinking and glancing. The girl who's taken a chair at the other end of my table keeps looking at me as if she's about to say something obscene. The air is dense. It's hard to breathe.

When I return from breakfast, I can't go into my room. The door handle has become a silver orb with sinister powers. I can't move. People try to help, but I'm dead, unreachable, under the power of the orb.

It's all part of a huge, impossible problem I have to solve. But my head is full of noise coming from somewhere else, breaking into my thoughts and replacing them with threats, coded messages, commentary. This noise hates me. In some part of myself, I'm aware of it coming out of my mouth and the bizarre faces of people pressing in on me.

The next thing I know, I'm lying on a bed in a hospital ward. I don't know how I got here or how long I've been here. A doctor in a white coat is holding up a needle, preparing to inject me. A nurse stands to the side of a trolley that supports a rectangular black box with dials and cords. I recognise it from the last time this happened, four years ago. It's the machine they use for electroconvulsive therapy. As I watch a second doctor adjust the knobs, I realise you don't die once only. Death is not a one-off event.

***

I tell them I've been raped. Mind rape. But they don't want to know.

I sit on the couch in the day room, my arms wrapped around my chest, holding myself tight, trying to cope with the pressure of the thoughts and images behind my eyes. I'm trapped in the underbelly of the mind, tormented by a relentless monologue. Words with no reason to be here. *Red mud blood, thick wet blood, red, shit oh shit, the bastard horror, take it off, idiot, off.* My head is full of this noise; spiders dance on my skin, electricity surges along my nerves. The sensations in my body are unbearable. A huge spider is crouching on my hair, crushing my head with its legs, laying eggs in my brain.

All I know for sure is that I'm Julianne and I'm dead.

My life has disappeared; no one recognises me for who I am. While my family members and friends seem familiar, I don't really know them. I'm Julianne. *But who am I to tell me who I am?* There are no words to say what my life is like: the thoughts that attack me, or the way that curtains and electric lights are possessed by threatening powers. The safety net of language has holes in it, and I've fallen through. Whenever people visit me, someone starts speaking in tongues. I don't know if it's me or them. Words are potent and hostile. Language betrays me, and people's faces are carnival masks of confusion and distrust. Eyebrows especially catch my attention. They are the face's punctuation marks, signing off on the threat in the eyes. I can't look. I turn away.

Attending to my existence takes all my attention as I defend myself against chaos in sleepless dreams of war. Images from films, books and visits to the Australian War Memorial torment me: Pozières where my grandfather lost his leg, Auschwitz, Hiroshima, My Lai. Visions of battlefields. Word grenades exploding in my head. The cries of dying men. My grandfathers in the trenches of the Western Front. Bodies of concentration camp inmates. I'm in a ward or a war – I can't think which, or what the difference might be.

When nurses respond in their firm way to my erratic behaviour, I'm sure they're going to kill me. When I'm particularly agitated, I'm held facedown on the bed, pants pulled low so they can inject me with a tranquilliser.

Turn off, turn off, stand up, up, orders from headquarters, the head's exploding, the head, someone's pulled the plug.

At times I'm taken to the locked isolation room: a small cell-like room with a mattress on the floor and a square peephole in the door but no handle. High on one wall is an oblong window. Whenever I look up, a rectangle of light moves towards me, becoming bigger and more intense as it approaches. *What does it mean? Where is the undertaker?*

Every second day after a night of thirst and fasting, they come and take me to the female dormitory, used in the mornings for ECT. The beds are stripped to the undersheet. The anaesthetist in his white coat stands at the end of the bed beside the ECT machine. Something plastic is pushed inside my mouth. Gel is placed on my temples. Then I'm dragged under, into unconsciousness.

There are no eyes here.

I'm Persephone, abducted by Hades into the underworld. I'm dead, and nothing will ever be the same again.

***

doctor says how are you today
I say, am I today
he says, we'll start another
series of ECT treatments on Monday
I say, another series of ECT
he says, you responded
well to the last lot
I say, the last lot
he says, that's
all for this week

can't get up from the chair
so he gets two nurses who
pull me up and steer me out
one says, is anything wrong
I say, wrong
the other one says
here's your medication
and I swallow the pills

I have conflicting attitudes to the medication. There are days I would swallow any drug available, take anything at all, to get rid of the chaos. At other times I'm suspicious, sure that the drugs and the ECT will kill me. So I pretend to take the pills, then spit them out later. The psychiatrist says that the treatment will silence the noise in my head but, instead, it silences me.

The hospital staff move as if they don't want to be here. They're not unkind, though; at times they're sympathetic, and there's a moment of contact, a shared understanding. The exception is Sister G, a middle-aged woman with a jutting chin and thin lips, a sharp tongue, and a uniform that's belted tight around her waist. She can be nasty and she sees everything. She seems to believe her job is to obey a system that considers us a management problem. When she's off duty, the place relaxes; sometimes, down the corridor, the nurses can be heard chatting and laughing together.

The passing of time is marked by medication rituals, doctors' appointments, visiting hours, and bells that announce meals. When the nurses bring in the medication trolley, we line up like communicants to receive a cup of water and a smaller paper cup containing our syrup or pills. We each take a mouthful of the water and swallow the drugs, watched intently by the senior nurse. Afterwards, one by one, we turn away from the line, crush the containers in our hands, and throw them in the bin. The ceremony is complete. We go back to our place at a table or around the edges of the day room, sedated and tranquillised, returned to our personal agonies.

Some patients talk to one another, but mostly we're locked away in our isolated and isolating inner worlds. Group therapy is held to get us talking, but it's a torturous experience that just leaves me feeling even more remote from other patients. We tend to avoid eye contact, staring into the distance or pacing around the day room and along the corridor. We see ourselves in one another and want to keep our distance, respectful of our shared need for privacy.

One night, I'm sitting in the day room writing in my notebook when I look at a patient leaning against the wall. I notice his hand going back and forth repetitively from his forehead to his nose to his mouth to his chest. As I watch, I realise it's not me who is looking. It's the mind behind the eyes that's doing the looking. And I'm not my mind.

I see that the mind has no identity. It's an abstract thing, disconnected from me, with its own agenda. Glacial and remote, it takes note of every detail. It is utterly foreign. Extraterrestrial. It sees the bone structure beneath people's faces, the glinting light on the scissors in the nurse's top pocket, the dregs in the coffee cup. But the mind will not disclose to me the meaning of what it sees.

I can't understand what anything means.

***

As the days of waiting circle around one another, fragmentary memories of Julianne emerge. I glance up from my dinner and see her on the chair opposite, looking at me with a half-smile, and a rush of joy or pain – I can't tell which – tears through my chest. Another time, coming into my room, I see her bend over to pick up her bag, and I notice the delicacy of her hands and the softness of her hair as it falls across her face. Sometimes I hear her say things like 'pass me that book' or 'let's take the bus'. I'm upset by these visitations, but as soon as she disappears I want her back.

Seeing and hearing Julianne external to myself challenges my belief that I'm her and brings on a new series of anxieties. Without her identity, who am I? If I'm not my mind and I'm not Julianne, where have I gone?

In the day room, I think of Julianne as she was the first time I saw her. The memory erupts full-blown, and I'm transported back in time. I'm twelve years old, sitting at my desk at the back of the first form classroom. Julianne is standing still and alert to the side of two nuns: our headmistress, Sister Clare, and our form teacher, Mother Aloysius. Wearing the brown uniform of her previous school and holding her head at an angle, Julianne has the look of a deer that has just stepped out of a forest into a clearing. There is a sense of space around her, a quiet poise, and I'm curious. When Sister Clare introduces her as the oldest of six children and French on her mother's side, Julianne looks out the window and frowns. She's in another world; her eyes are distant and squinting slightly, as if she's thinking of a problem she needs to solve.

Back in M Ward the classroom retreats, but Julianne is still standing in front of me with the same thoughtful look. I'm unable to bear the sight of her, so much herself, so real and present that I want to shake her, wake her up. I also want her to go; she doesn't exist. But when she leaves, I'm desperate with self-reproach. *Where? Where, ma chère amie? Tu es un pomme, je suis une poire, tu es trop drôle, disparu, disparu.* I beat my chest hard with my fist until my ribs ache. A nurse comes, gives me water and pills, and helps me walk along the corridor to my room.

***

The next day I'm in 'death's dream kingdom' again, almost blind from the cold and the loneliness. I'm a mannequin-ghost haunting the ward, my skin pulled tight across my bones, careful not to let my eyes give anything away. Sitting back on a couch in the day room, my legs crossed, I lift my cigarette to my mouth, take a drag, then exhale slowly and look around through the smoke. My eyes see everything, every little thing: the servitude of the chairs as they wait at the tables, so patient and receptive. The weight of the shuffling bodies as they move across the floor to the kitchen alcove. The light grazing the green lino. And all the angles that cut into the space around me: ceiling, walls, windows. Sharp and decisive. Too much information. No meaning. No pattern.

I'm numb and deeply sedated. The noise inside my head has grown less strident, and the hallucinations of war are less explosive. But I still can't convince myself that I'm alive.

There are rules for everything, and everyone except me knows what they are – how to arrange your face, when to say certain things, what to do when someone looks at you. These rules enable people to act without having to think it through. But no intuition or knowledge emerges to direct me, so every interaction is fraught. I have become a thing that can't see the connections between things. I write in my notebook:

energy of ages

boring holes in my skull
where eyes would be
if only I could see

My mind is white and cold. I've lost my soul. I am a moth. I'm no one.

That night I slip out the door of the ward and make my way through the hospital grounds to the shore of Lake Burley Griffin. Gum trees and pines loom in the darkness along each side of the track and, ahead of me, reflections of hospital lights shine like pieces of broken crystal on the surface of the water.

I've lived my life and now it's over. This is where it has brought me, face to face with yet another death. I know it for what it is, and I'm ready to embrace it fully. I'll be Ned Kelly in Nolan's painting, turn my back on this world and ride into infinity. I've never wanted anything as much as I want this life to end. I want to become sky. Become nothing. I pace along the path next to the stone wall on the lake's edge with only one thought in my mind: to drown, to do something that will make sense of it all. No longer dead as Julianne, I'm now dead as myself, and I can't bear it for even one more night.

I stand motionless on the edge of the lake, imagining how it will feel to let the dark water close over me as I sink to the bottom: the peace, the quiet, the letting go under the weight of the water. The fantasy grips me, and I lose touch with myself entirely.

Then a water rat runs across my foot. I'm wearing sandals, and the sensation of claws on my skin is revolting. The shock of it brings me back to the reality of the night.

I look again into the water, but this time I gauge its depth. It wouldn't be that easy to drown. I'm a strong swimmer. The instinct to save myself, to rise to the surface, will take over. The shore is right here.

There's no way out after all. I turn around and make my way back to M Ward. I'm worthless, pared down to nothing. I've come to the very end of possibility.

2

Make Love Not War

It's midnight and I'm sitting in the semi-darkness of the day room. Traces of the day's failures and worries cling to the shadows. Near the door, a fluorescent light flickers and buzzes like a trapped insect. The other patients are asleep, and the few staff working the graveyard shift have retreated to the nurses' station. I've been here since the last visitors filed out the door, trying to deflect the noise in my head by writing in my notebook. Breathing in and out. Hanging on.

The door swings open, and three people spill into the room. A tall young man falls to his knees. He's pitched forward with his head down as though carrying a weight on his shoulders. I recognise the scene immediately: it's the Stations of the Cross, the ninth, 'Jesus Falls the Third Time'. In the dim light, I see two orderlies in white bend to take his arms and help him up. There's a formal tenderness in their movements, an unhurried attention that the young man's body seems to respond to despite its weakness. With the orderlies supporting him on either side, the three move slowly into the corridor, a hessian bag trailing along the floor behind them.

The young man has long hair, a frizzy mass that curls over his shoulders, and he's wearing jeans, a loose shirt and boots. His arms are slung across the shoulders of the orderlies, and his feet stumble, unable to bear his weight. As the trio passes by a wall light, I see that the young man's glasses are broken, hanging at an angle halfway down his face.

I watch as this odd procession makes its way along the corridor and out of sight. I go back to my notebook, disturbed, wondering if this scene was real.

***

A couple of days later, I'm in the day room with the other patients, eating breakfast. We slouch in and out of the kitchen alcove, making coffee and toast, and pouring cereal into bowls. No one is properly awake. No one speaks. With the clutter of cutlery and music from the radio in the background, we drift in a half-sleep, our movements automatic, each mind a cocoon. I'm sitting alone, spooning Weet-Bix into my mouth while trying to ignore the whispers that appear in my head like erratic blips on a radar.

When I notice someone standing opposite me, I look up. It's the Stations of the Cross man, silhouetted by the light from the window behind him. I'd begun to believe I imagined him, but I see now that he's definitely real, and very thin and tall. Smiling in a slightly unfocused, lopsided way.

'Mind if I sit here?' His voice has a higher pitch than I expected, and it makes me think of delicate china.

I look away, surprised and wary. I'm no longer used to being approached or addressed so directly.

He folds his long body into a chair opposite me and introduces himself as Michael. I stare at my soggy Weet-Bix while he launches into a good-natured commentary on the cereal options in M Ward. Leaning forward in his chair, he's happy to keep talking in spite of my silence. 'I've been staying on a farm just past Tharwa,' he says. 'A place called Caloola. Sheep country. I've been helping with the lambing, doing odd jobs. It's a refuge for city junkies.'

'Oh, right,' I say, at length. I have no idea how to respond.

'I'm coming off heroin. It's been a bad scene. I'm here to get help with the withdrawals.'

'I know,' I say, although I don't. What I mean is, his weakness the other night now makes sense. I check out the door. Even though he's across the table, he feels too close. I want more space between us.

'How long have you been here?' he asks.

'I'm not sure,' I say as I continue eating. I have no idea what day of the week it is, what month. My mother told me yesterday I've been here just over a week, but I feel as if I've never been anywhere else. What is a week? How would you explain time?

He looks away and is quiet for a while. Eventually the silence is interrupted by a patient at another table humming loudly. 'That's the guy in my dorm who sings in his sleep,' Michael says. 'He's not bad. I'm thinking of putting together a band he can front.' His eyes are teasing, and he's leaning forward even further, smiling.

'The Nocturnals,' I murmur, liking him now.

'Lead singer, Insomnia,' he says.

'Mania on drums,' I reply.

Michael giggles, a high rippling sound, and pulls his fingers through his wispy beard. I stare at him and see that he's an elf, a tall elf.

'So, what're you in for?' he asks.

I watch him reach for a piece of toast and wonder if there's a crime I can name, some felony that can explain it all away.

'I'm dead,' I say.

'What does that feel like?'

I look sideways, my mind a blank. 'Ash,' I say at last. 'It feels like ash.'

'Sounds bleak,' he replies, leaning back in his chair. He strokes his beard again and looks around the room. 'So this is bardo country,' he says, as though to himself. 'I should've guessed.'

'Yes,' I say, recognising the allusion. 'Death's dream kingdom.'

I've read *The Tibetan Book of the Dead* and know that the bardo is the realm where the soul goes after death, a state of transition before rebirth. Michael's reference is like a revelation, turning a key in my mind: of course, I'm in bardo country. *In this valley of dying stars.* I'm waiting to be born again.

This strange man sitting opposite me seems to understand what it's like to die. Now it's important that I talk to him. I sit up and push my hair back from my face.

He coughs once, then again. Suddenly his whole body is given over to a fit of harsh, racking coughs. He turns on his chair and heaves with the effort of coughing and the need to gasp for breath between each attack. I look away until they subside, feeling his discomfort. 'Chronic bronchitis,' he explains. His eyes are watering and his face is grey. 'I need to take the cure.'

An ironic smile invites me to make light of his predicament, and I find myself smiling in response.

'Hey, listen to that,' he says, his arm gesturing towards the stereo. 'It's Vivaldi. Want to come and listen?'

I have my own recording of Vivaldi's *The Four Seasons* in my room, and I take this as another sign that I need to work out who this man is. I leave the table with him, and we find a place on the floor next to the speakers. He sits cross-legged opposite me and takes out a box of unfiltered Camels from his shirt pocket. He offers me one, but I prefer my own and roll myself a cigarette from my tobacco pouch. We sit there listening to the music together, sipping our coffee and smoking. I look at his hands. They are long and freckled, and, in contrast to the fragility of the rest of his body, they give the impression of strength. Brown tobacco stains smudge his fingertips, and a silver ring on his little finger is engraved with some sort of crest.

Sitting so close to the speakers with the sound turned up high, I sense his profound attention to the music. I think of his first appearance on the ward, and an uncanny feeling of intimacy surfaces. I'm aware of myself tuning in to him, listening through his listening. The static and noise inside my head gives way to the sound of violins, and music fills the room like a flock of small birds, dipping and weaving. I close my eyes and sink into myself. For the first time since I've come to the ward, I feel my breath as my own.

After the music stops, Michael smiles at me as if we're both in on a secret. He stretches out his legs and leans back against the wall, quiet and relaxed. I roll another cigarette, and we begin a conversation that's wide open and frayed at the edges, easy to drift in and out of. During one of the pauses, he reads a record cover. I note his wayward hair, his fine features, and the rimless glasses askew on his face.

It occurs to me that I've seen him before, in a Rembrandt painting of a youth with a soft beard and a narrow, birdlike neck. We begin to talk of poetry and our favourite poets. He adjusts his broken glasses and tells me that his full name is Michael Dransfield. He says he's a poet.

It makes absolute sense, but such a claim, such audacity: 'I'm a poet.'

With this statement – straight to the core of his being, without ego or pretence – something falls into place for me. I believe him utterly and look even more closely. He seems to have the sensibility of a poet. He is perceptive and responsive, and he listens to music as if it's coming from deep inside him. I want to read his poems.

***

After lunch we go into my room, closing the door behind us, and I'm grateful for the privacy. I have been given a room to myself because I'm restless at night and pace the ward. The room is just big enough for an upright chair, a single bed and a bedside table attached to a narrow wardrobe. There's also an easy chair next to the window that looks out to the brick wall of a storage building. Clothes are scattered around, and my cream-and-maroon portable record player sits on the floor next to a pile of records.

On the bedside table, a vase of sweet peas finds a place among a few books: collections of the poetry of T.S. Eliot and

Judith Wright, and a book of Japanese poetry that Julianne gave me. I find their presence comforting, although I can barely read them. The medication I'm on affects my eyes, making it difficult to focus. I have to squint to see text, so it's impossible to read more than one short poem at a time.

I sit on my bed while Michael examines my books and records, holding them up close to his eyes as he reads the titles and skims through pages. He opens the book of Japanese poetry and reads the inscription aloud:

> *This lovely afternoon,*
> *Time hanging heavy on my hands*
> *Comes a visitor like a jewel out of the sands.*
> *Pour ma chérie, Paula, meilleure amie pour la vie,*
> *love, Julianne.*

Michael looks at me and smiles. 'Who's Julianne?'

'A friend,' I say. 'From school.'

My words feel like a dismissal. Like rubbish being thrown away. Michael says nothing. I look back at him, standing with the book in his hands and the question still in his eyes. In the silence between us, I long to hear myself say something true, words that would end my isolation.

The room grows large with absence. As if from a distance, I see Michael arrange his long frame on the chair by the window and start reading the book. Gradually my breathing becomes less of an effort, and grief recedes back to where it has lain since Julianne died. I'm relieved that Michael is so immersed in the book that he seems to have forgotten I'm here. His body is a geometrical puzzle of limbs, and sunlight shines through his hair, forming a lacework corona around his head. With his glasses and his smile, and his moustache and wispy beard, there's both a shininess and featheriness about him. When he moves, he has the grace of a long-legged water bird, a heron or a crane.

The door opens, and a nurse appears. 'What's going on in here?' she says, standing with one hand on her hip and the other on the doorknob. I jump, startled, and immediately feel guilty and defensive. But Michael just gestures towards the nurse, as if bestowing a blessing on her, then turns to me and rolls his eyes. We recognise that although we're voluntary patients, our time on the ward will be monitored.

With the door wide open now and noise from the corridor in the background, we begin a conversation. The fine tones of Michael's voice are punctuated at times by a high, nervous giggle. I'm aware of his frailty and his cough, and I watch the way light and shadow play across his eyes as he speaks. We talk about poetry and listen to Bob Dylan and Vivaldi, and I am freed for a while from the violence of the noise.

As we talk, Michael and I seamlessly enter each other's worlds. There's an underwater quality to the room and to our conversation, as if we're submerged in a deep stream, a meandering flow of language that carries us along. With Michael, there's no need to translate or decode; the energy of ideas bursts through in a play of open speech. We're swimming together, rising on currents, gliding through clear water. An exhilarated cutting loose. And somehow also an anchoring, each with the other.

The afternoon drifts, and I fall easily, inevitably, into love. Into a dream of love. Into his blue eyes, his otherworldliness and gentle presence. Everything about him. The way he remains attentive during the silences in our conversation, as if silence is a special form of communication. His manner of speaking; his private school accent threaded through with 1960s Americanisms and Australian slang. The way his eyes almost close when he smiles, and I look for it, wondering if anyone else has noticed that in him.

Michael has walked into my life like someone with a message for me. I see him sitting by the window, gesturing as he speaks, his smile quick and impish – and everything he says is something I need to hear. I want to ask him to read some of his poems aloud but feel this would be an intrusion. So I imagine him reading. His voice is of air and breath and walking.

***

Except for sleeping, Michael and I are inseparable. Each morning we meet in the day room over breakfast and compare our nights spent apart; the dreams and poems, the sleepless thoughts and wonderings. Only after this reunion can we move into the day together. We make trips to the cafeteria in the general hospital for coffee and stroll to the mailroom to collect Michael's letters.

As we sit at a corner table of the cafeteria, Michael holds my hand in both of his and tells me that he loves me. 'Last night I wrote five new poems,' he says, smiling, his head at an angle.

We've known each other for three days. I smile. I love him too. I tell him, and it feels like the most amazing thing I've ever said.

The next morning Michael and I search the lake shore for somewhere calm and private. Sunlight plays on the water and small boats sail in the distance as we make our way along the path, scattering ducks as we go. Taking a turn, we catch sight of a weeping willow sweeping the ground and, further out, bending into the water at the edge of the lake. I sense we've found our refuge.

Michael pulls aside the branches, and we walk into a room of filtered light, a round space enclosed by cascading greenery. For a moment we stand there, quiet, our eyes adjusting to the shade. Then Michael says, 'It's a green bell,' and repeats the willow's Latin name, *'Salix babylonica,'* as if it were a prayer, an invocation. I think of the Hanging Gardens of Babylon, remembering from childhood a picture of their arching vaults and climbing terraces. The drapery of leaves, the play of light and shadow.

We sit on a bare patch of ground and settle in. Michael has his arm around me, and I lean into his musky warmth, listening to the lapping of the lake on the shore, the warbling of magpies from the trees behind us, the distant hum of hospital machinery. Sunlight filters through the soft down of new growth, and long tendrils of leaves hang around us like sheer curtains, protecting us in our secret green idyll.

As I notice the faint smell of water reeds and duck droppings, I remember as a child collecting eggs from the chook house in the early morning. I would stand quite still, breathing in the odour of damp straw as I held a warm, full egg in the cradle of my hand. With this memory, the minds within my mind retreat. The air is mellow, easy to breathe, soothing. Jangling nerves are humbled, and gratitude eases into each breath.

Michael lights my cigarette and then his own. The mood is slow and quiet as we smoke and talk about our favourite trees. I describe a dinosaur-like Moreton Bay fig I climbed in the Sydney Botanical Gardens when I was a child, and Michael laughs about a blue gum he planted in an inner-city backyard, speculating about its height and whether or not it has survived. Casuarinas that grow along the Cotter River and rows of poplars on the road to Cooma link to more anecdotes, while wattles, elms and Japanese maples play on the edges of this arboreal litany. We agree, though, that despite all their qualities, none is as sublime as this green willow bell.

We're truly alone together for the first time, and I'm aware of the sexual tension in the air. I trace the outline of Michael's lips with the tip of my finger and imagine the taste of him. It seems absurd to me that I'm inside a green bell about to kiss a man whose smile is like music. I laugh at the thought of it, and that's when he draws me to him.

Eventually we realise that we've been away from the ward longer than we should. We walk back through the trees, arm in arm, rippling with happiness.

***

Michael writes down poems as they come to him, wherever we are. Once, when we're leaving the mailroom, he writes a poem on the envelope of an unopened letter. We talk about his poetry, and he tells me that three books of his poems have been published and a fourth has been sent to some publishers. Writing poetry is more than a daily practice for Michael – it's his passion, the core of who he is.

We're still getting to know each other. We establish that we're both Virgos, born a year apart and grown up in the suburbs – Michael in Brighton-Le-Sands, Sydney. He tells me about his father who died last year, and his mother, Elspeth, and sister, Frances, who still live in Sydney. He describes his ancestral connections to the Russian aristocracy, and to titled families in Poland and Czechoslovakia. He shows me his ring, engraved with the family crest, and gives it to me to try on, to feel the weight of it.

He also describes himself as sixth-generation Australian, descended from pioneering country people who lived on the south coast of New South Wales. In his personal dreaming, Michael sees himself as the child of both high European culture and rural Australia. He's entranced by European music, poetry and traditions, but he also prides himself on his connection to farmers: down-to-earth, fair dinkum people who work hard and live simply, without pretensions to grandeur and wealth.

I tell Michael of my experiences with Catholicism, the wars my father and grandfathers fought, and my mother's stories about the Great Depression. These are my defining cultural imprints. Like Michael, I'm sixth-generation Australian, but descended from Irish Catholics who settled in Sydney: Hanlons, Sullivans and Hennessys, as well as Keoghs. My extended family were close during my early life, but after my parents moved us to Canberra when I was nine, contact was limited to the occasional holiday. Mine is a family of seven children: insular, exuberant and clannish.

I show Michael the poems I've written about my maternal grandfather fighting in France in World War

I, and he encourages me to write more. His grandfather also saw action during that war, and both our fathers fought in World War II. The way we see it, these family histories makes it all the more necessary for us to oppose the war in Vietnam. We believe that people our age must end the cycle of violence in which each generation of young men is sent away to killing fields across the world.

But in spite of the similarity of our backgrounds, Michael seems to be everything I'm not. Compared to his wild life of drugs and rebellion, mine has been tame. Many of his anecdotes have a heroic flavour – stories of himself as a rebel and adventurer, living like an outlaw on the edge of society. He talks of taking risks and getting high on whatever drugs he can find. 'I'm coming back as an eagle, flying high on the wind, seeing for miles,' he says. 'The Celtic name for eagle means "eye of the sun". Cool, eh?'

At other moments he's nostalgic, talking of his need to escape the claustrophobia of the city and take off into the country. In colourful details, he describes the two properties he bought in the New South Wales countryside: a beautiful old Cobargo house called Marchpane that he no longer owns, and a small acreage near Candelo called Jumping Creek with a stone cottage surrounded by grazing cattle.

After telling me about these idyllic places, Michael shifts back to his enthusiastic accounts of drug taking. I know Alan Ginsberg's poetry, and I've read about the ideas of gurus like Timothy Leary and Richard Alpert, but I haven't been inspired to 'tune in, turn on, drop out'. My experiences of psychosis are too close, too disturbing. I tried marijuana a few times, but it made me anxious and fearful. I want an ordinary, everyday consciousness, one I can rely on to construct a reality that holds firm. And I want to be at university – I'm desperate to finish my studies.

Even so, I'm interested in Michael's descriptions of himself as a 'junkie'. I empathise with his desire for spiritual and artistic breakthroughs, and when he speaks of how drugs expand his mind, I'm curious. His descriptions of what happens when he takes drugs don't make it sound at all like being mad. He focuses on their pleasurable effects, talking about them like a zealot. They are, for him, a source of creativity and insight.

'But you're here to get off drugs,' I say.

'Yeah, right,' he says, grinning. 'Had too much of a good thing.'

***

I have an appointment today with the psychiatrist. I take quick glimpses of him as I sit in my chair in front of his desk. As usual, he's wearing a dark suit and a wide tie, and the horn-rimmed glasses that seem too small for his round face. I know that the nurses like him, but I can't see why. He seems detached and cold to me, and I don't trust him.

He tells me that another series of ECT treatments will be conducted. I nod. He says he's changing my medication to include something stronger to help me sleep. I nod again. I'm now able to accept that the intention in M Ward is not to kill me. I understand that the aim of the psychiatrists is to eradicate the madness in me. The problem is that the treatments destroy my spirit, my passion, my soul. Then again, so does the madness.

The psychiatrist who treats me is called Doctor Hawke. The nurses say he is 'my psychiatrist' but I can't use that term. It connects me to him in a way I can't bear. His name is also a problem, and I don't like to use it to refer to him. It doesn't feel true to me. The thing is, hawks are magnificent birds: proud, intelligent, beautiful, and they have amazing eyesight. They can see eight times better than humans. I look at the psychiatrist's eyes, and they see nothing. I sit here, five feet away from him, and he doesn't see me. He sees symptoms. To him, I'm just a case of schizophrenia, a disease that has to be eliminated. As a person, I'm ignored, my questions are brushed aside, and when I try to understand what's happening to me from within my strange and estranged reality, I'm silenced.

As far as the psychiatrist is concerned, I have a chemical imbalance in my brain and that's that. The answer is ECT and medication. I'm totally left out of the equation.

Michael has a different experience of his psychiatrist, a sympathetic and responsive man. But Michael doesn't have much faith in the treatments. He's also frustrated by the way some people react to him, as if being a junkie and a hippie makes him less deserving of medical support. A few staff members clearly believe that his illness is self-inflicted and that he isn't entitled to the treatment other patients are getting. Sister G is openly contemptuous of Michael. Whenever she sees him, she becomes as stiff and tight as a military officer. And when she comes across the two of us, she makes a tutting sound through her teeth before turning away on her heels. Her prejudice is directed not only at Michael but also at Andy, another recovering drug addict.

Michael doesn't want to be in M Ward, and neither do I, but we can't cope out in the world. We feel we have no choice but to stay in the hospital and hope that we can somehow come through to health and sanity.

***

Michael believes that the earth is dying – this is a reality for him, one he carries like a wound. When he talks about the effects of oil spills or pollution, or the Vietnam War, he turns inward. There's a sense of helplessness then, and only his dark humour gets us through. He becomes ironic, aware that the same old conversations won't help anything.

We're sitting with some other patients at a table in the day room when the discussion turns to Vietnam.

'You lot don't know what you're talkin' about,' says the Man from Kosciuszko. 'If it weren't for our troops in New Guinea, this country would be run by the Japs now. We've got to defend Australia, stop the Viet Cong before they get here.'

'This is a different war, different situation,' says Andy. 'The Viet Cong aren't interested in invading Australia. It's a war within their own country. We should let them sort it out themselves. Vietnam for the Vietnamese.'

'What do you reckon, Mick?' says the Man from Kosciuszko. He never calls Michael by his full name. 'How are we going to stop those bloody Viet Cong from invading Australia?'

'You don't have to ask what he thinks about the war,' says Andy. 'It'd be obvious, wouldn't it?'

'You'd probably have to do something pretty extreme to stop the Viet Cong,' Michael says thoughtfully, glancing at me with a wicked gleam in his eye. 'Probably need chemical warfare.'

'You're joking,' says Andy, grinning.

'You reckon?' says Michael. 'You'd need to get Dow Chemicals or maybe Monsanto to make a really toxic herbicide, give it a cool name, maybe "Agent Orange", and drop it all over the country. Maximum damage.'

He takes a long drag on his cigarette. 'Yeah, chemical warfare would be the way to go. Poison everyone in the area – pity about the civilians, the women and the kids, but, hell, that's war. And it'll destroy the crops too, so if people aren't already dead from the toxicity of the stuff, they'll starve to death. You'd contaminate the rivers and kill off the forests at the same time. Let those commie Viet Cong know you mean business. Call it "war". Say we're defending Australia.'

Michael stubs out his cigarette in an ashtray and speaks quietly, in an offhand way. 'Agent Orange is chemical warfare and it's been used for years in Vietnam by the Yanks, and probably by us too. But the Viet Cong aren't going away.'

'Ah, you think you've got it all worked out,' says the Man from Kosciuszko, pointing his finger at Michael. 'But you have no idea what it takes to win a war.'

'Yeah, well, maybe not,' says Michael. He sounds weary. He raises one hand and makes the peace sign. 'Hey, man, make love not war.' As he gets up to go into the kitchen, he asks the Man from Kosciuszko if he wants another coffee.

***

Since Michael's arrival, I've become more aware of the existence of other patients. Sitting around the day room, Michael will often strike up conversations, drawing people out, interested to hear their stories or just chat.

We've quickly befriended Kate McNamara, a student who was at university in Sydney. I am in awe of her. She has wild blonde hair and sea-blue eyes behind red-framed glasses. When she speaks, you know she's speaking her truth. She says exactly what she thinks and doesn't care what people think of her. She is a goddess woman. She lives at the extremities of experience and jokes about it. Writes poems that take you there.

I can now see how much I have in common with the other patients. In our different ways, we're in extreme states – lost, displaced and unhinged.

I'm distracted by a boy of about fifteen who stalks along the corridor and around the day room, muttering, his shoulders hunched, his eyes darting. I think of him as the ward sentry. To him, everything that happens signifies a threat. I see him pacing, encased in isolation, churning with anxiety, and I turn away, unable to bear his desperation.

We're all dealing with uncertain levels of control. Yesterday, an older man exposed himself to a female patient who was wandering near the male dormitory. She taunted him, 'Okay, you've got it out, now what are ya gonna do with it?' She screamed with laughter and pretended to tear open her shirt.

A tall woman, Lydia, occasionally explodes with paranoid accusations against anyone in her vicinity. She has thick black hair and disturbing Frida Kahlo eyebrows. She thinks she's the ward prefect and takes it on herself to make sure everyone behaves themselves. 'Lustful hands are the devil's work,' she says any time she catches Michael and I hand in hand or sitting close together on a couch.

Then there's a pale woman who sits alone in the day room staring into the distance, sometimes crying. She looks cold even though she wears a thick, oversized cardigan, her pockets stuffed with handkerchiefs. Every evening a man in a suit arrives and sits with her, holding her hand, occasionally stroking it. His briefcase contains photos and cards that he takes out to show her, one by one. He speaks softly, but she rarely responds. I always feel defeated when he leaves, as if I'm somehow responsible for the sadness in the slope of his shoulders as he slips out the door.

***

One afternoon, resting together in the green bell, Michael and I talk about our childhoods. We're excited when we discover that we both listened to the ABC children's radio program *The Argonauts.* I feel as if we know the password to the child in each other.

'Do you remember the song? "Fifty mighty Argonauts–"' Michael begins.

'"–bending to the oars",' I join in.

'"Good rowing!" Shit, I loved that program, Pauls.'

The Argonauts presented segments covering geography, history and the arts. It introduced me to the idea that children could make up stories and write poetry. Based on the Greek myth of Jason and the Golden Fleece, it encouraged the romantic idea that life is an adventure, a heroic journey, a sea voyage in pursuit of a cherished goal. With your fellow Argonauts, you brave the dangers that beset you along the way and stay on course, until you retrieve your inheritance, the golden fleece.

The discovery of this piece of shared history proves to me and Michael that we are kindred spirits, fated to meet.

Talking to Michael, I see my childhood in a new light. I never felt free as a child to express my ideas or my feelings. Although we had a great deal of physical freedom to explore and wander, freedom of expression wasn't valued. Existence was something to be earned, minute by minute, by being good, being obedient, being pure. Sin had to be avoided at all costs, so I lit candles in front of the statue of Our Lady, and I worshipped at the altar of a God nailed to a cross and crowned with thorns.

For me, Catholicism was a religion of dark compulsions, dark mysteries, guilt and sin. The belief that God could see everything I did, hear every wicked thought, dominated all the small and large dramas of my childhood. In the wooden confessional, I admitted my sins to a shadowy figure behind the grille, desperate for my guilty soul to be wiped clean. The day of my First Confession I wet my pants as I knelt in the pew, waiting to confess something; I was seven years old and terrified of what would happen behind the wooden door. I knew my badness was much worse than the petty sins I confessed to, but I couldn't name it, so I couldn't be forgiven. It was nothing I did exactly, it was just something I was, and Confession could offer no relief. I prayed anxiously about everything, but especially I prayed to be good. I dreamed of being a nun.

At high school, there was an emphasis on intellectual questioning in subjects like literature and history, and on social issues such as capital punishment, but faith was seen as another category entirely. It transcended the intellect. Many of the nuns who taught us were inspiring women who modelled independent thought – except on matters of faith. Until Julianne and I went to university, it would have been very difficult for us to question Church doctrines. As a teenager, I believed deeply, unquestioningly, in God and His Church, and I wanted more than anything to be loved by Him and the people in my life.

With Michael, I've found the love I longed for. My heart is practically breaking with love for him – and the fact that he loves me is an epiphany. Whatever we're feeling, whatever is happening on the ward, we look to each other for reassurance and understanding. Even in the silences, we're listening to each other.

Our love is, for me, an initiation into a world free of guilt. A world where all that had once been sin – rebellion, wildness, pleasure – is now holy, almost sacramental.

From time to time, when I'm with Michael, I feel a flash of energy, a surge of confidence. I remember dancing at Dimitri's that Saturday night before my breakdown. Raising my arms high, stamping my foot down. A flare sent out from a past self.

3

Julianne

The noise in my head doesn't like me being happy. I wake up from a long, involved nightmare with the sensation of a spider's web covering my face and a stream of abuse filling my mind. *Slut idiot, slut bitch, ugly, turn the other cheek, check the other chart, the fires of hell, the hell fires.* It's early, long before breakfast time. I make my way to the day room and start writing in my notebook, trying to distract myself from the noise.

But there's something new, a sense of hope that I have when I'm with Michael, a light inside me that's not madness. It's so very small and fragile, though, a glow worm in a cave of bats, unable to withstand the noise as it increases in volume and ferocity. I stand up, knocking over my coffee in my rush to get back to my room.

As I pass the vacant nurses' station, a phone is ringing. And ringing.

Its call is insistent. I can't bear the sound. In my room, I throw myself on the bed and cover my ears. But the phone's still ringing.

It's four years earlier, and I'm standing at the phone table in the hall of my parents' house, not quite awake, holding the receiver in my hand. I hear Mrs Gilroy's voice and wonder why she would be calling so early. Then I feel myself bend forward, leaning on the table for support. Mrs Gilroy is saying that Julianne died in the night.

My mind becomes hollow. I hear the words but their meaning falls away. When I hang up the phone, my mother is standing in front of me, grasping her dressing-gown at her chest with one hand. I stare at her, trying to find words to tell her what has happened. Even as I say them, they make no sense to me. I turn and walk out the back door.

I run into the yard, thrust forward by a blind momentum. I cross the wet lawn and make my way towards the hooded shape of Mount Majura and the track into the bush. I'm conscious of every step and the icy air on my face. I hear birdcalls and breathe in the smell of earth. In the half-light, the tree trunks appear stark and grotesque, and stillness hangs in the air like a spell. I'm aware of my breath, sharp and tight, and the blood rushing through my body. I keep moving fast. The skin on my face is taut, my eyes are wide open, my breath is now coming in fierce surges, in and out.

When I pass a dam, the vegetation changes and I stop walking. The path ahead leads into a dense expanse of trees that seems remote and sinister. I stand quite still, struck by the strangeness of a place I know so well. Pink and orange light is splashed across the sky behind the dark form of the mountain.

In the silence, I hear myself think: *It's the first day of her death.*

The words are a shock. I'm back in M Ward. I look around my room and try to orientate myself. 'The first day of her death' is not an idea I can process. Although my mind refuses its meaning, my heart knows that Julianne is dead. I know I will never see her again. But I'm circling her death, circling and looking, trying to see, moving away then returning, as if I'm waiting for her to wake up and explain it all to me. Because her death is impossible. We never thought we would ever die.

***

When Mrs Gilroy rang, she asked me to help with the children, so after I returned from the bush, I rode my bike to the Gilroy home. I had automatically clicked into my helpful and positive mode, but it took me longer to react to things. I was following myself through the morning's events, unable to catch up. I helped the younger children get dressed while the older girls took care of breakfast. No one was hungry and no one had much to say. A large bowl of homemade yoghurt sat on the kitchen bench, catching the light from the window. So white and smooth and perfect in a blue porcelain bowl.

The children were resentful when it was time for them to go to school. They wanted to stay in the house together, but as neighbours and friends came to get them, they dragged themselves and their large schoolbags up the drive to the street, subdued and uncomprehending, one after the other.

The silence in the house felt brittle as glass. I wandered from room to room, holding on tightly to my singular existence. I picked up clothes and put them on beds; I stacked dishes in the sink. In the lounge room, I studied the framed photos along the top of the piano. Next to assorted family portraits – and one of her father, who had died a year earlier – there was a photo of Julianne. It was a black-and-white image of her looking directly into the camera lens with a serious expression, her eyes quizzical. 'Who are *you?*' she seemed to be asking, reversing the role of the camera, refusing to be the object of its gaze.

In another photo, she stood in line with some of her sisters, her expression thoughtful, somewhat wary, as if she had retreated to a contained and unyielding part of herself. This wasn't the Julianne I knew. I wanted her to come home. In the empty house I waited for her to come back from the swimming pool. I was sure she must be there, or at the library. She would walk in the door any minute. If I just waited long enough, she would come.

The phone in the Gilroy house rang a number of times that morning. I answered it and listened while people expressed shock and disbelief, then I told each one what news I had, that a notice would be placed in the paper regarding the time of the funeral.

Sometime in the afternoon I went home. I had an essay to write about the influence of Ludwig Feuerbach's philosophy on the early writings of Marx. I found the ritual of writing a relief from the pressure in my chest. I went through my notes and made points for the essay plan. I worked on the introduction and came up with my argument, drawing on discussions Julianne and I had engaged in as our belief in God had collapsed. We'd talked about Feuerbach's idea that God is a product of human longings and wishes, and I wrote about how this idea had influenced Marx's ideas on religion. It became urgent that I finish the essay, which was due the following week.

That evening, sitting at the table having dinner with my family, I looked at the slices of bread on a plate and found them incomprehensible. I couldn't think of the word 'bread', only the word 'companion', a word that Julianne and I had particularly liked. At school, we had been obsessed with finding the derivations of words and had discovered that 'companion' is derived from the Old French, meaning 'with bread'. We decided that we were companions. We broke bread together. I sat there at the table, staring at the bread, unable to think of anything but the word 'companion', unable to look away.

My family were quiet, the conversation subdued. My mother had hugged me earlier and offered sympathy, but I was unused to displays of affection and didn't respond. No one mentioned Julianne. No one, including me, knew what to say.

***

Michael appears at my door, interrupting my memories of that stunned day. He's smiling, saying something about breakfast and offering his hand to help me up from the bed. We walk down the corridor to the day room, but I can't speak. I can't even look at him. *It's the first day of her death.* When breakfast is served, I eat. When the medication trolley comes around, I take the pills and syrup and swallow them. But throughout the morning, I'm mute, skeletal with grief.

Later, I sit on a couch staring straight ahead at the wall, aware of Michael sitting by my side. I know when he's taking a drag on a cigarette, turning a page of his notebook or sipping his coffee. I hear him say things, but it's the sound of his voice that makes sense to me, not the meaning of his words.

Someone has put a record on, and 'Danny Boy' is playing. 'It's you,' the voice sings. 'It's you must go, and I must bide.' Tears roll down my cheeks.

I nap in my room during the afternoon and wake to see Michael perched on the chair under the window. 'You've been asleep,' he says, putting down a book.

I sit up and try to think where I am. Try to remember who this person is.

'It's late afternoon,' he says. 'Time for Chopin.' He shows me the cover of the record he has put on my portable stereo. 'I nicked this from the day room,' he says.

While the light fades and shadows creep up the walls of my room, we sit together, feeling the melancholy in the music.

'Some things can't be said,' Michael says as he turns the record over. 'But then there's Chopin.'

As if on cue, there's a banging on the half-open door, and a nurse appears. She says it's time to go to the day room.

***

Different realities coexist in me like a set of Russian dolls. Except that the dolls inside me are all talking at the same time, feeling contrary emotions, seeing intersecting images that won't stay still. Loud monologues persist, mocking and sneering. It's all a confusion of impressions, sensations, feelings, faces. Or sounds, music, voices, noise. Hands gesturing. Eyebrows insinuating. The past inside the present inside the future. Love and death and all the imaginings, a mish-mash. They're all real and they're all mad. Truth and lies competing with one another for my mind.

This is my madness, and I can't tell it as it is. Madness is anti-story, anti-chronology, anti-plot, anti-character. It breaks language. It throws mud in the face. It makes story impossible. The minds within the mind won't let me be.

Even so, I move, I act, and my story continues. The body's truth with its red heart, and a mouth that wants to speak, urges me on.

***

'What was Julianne like?' Michael asks.

It's late at night, and there's no one else in the dimly lit day room. We're sitting together on a couch again, enjoying the opportunity to be physically close in private. I feel the weight of his arm around my shoulders and the delicate sensation of his fingers playing with hair at the nape of my neck.

'Julianne liked thinking,' I say slowly. 'And languages. When we were twelve she told me her goals in life were to speak French fluently and live in Paris.' I pause for a moment. 'And she was bold.' The word comes to me unexpectedly. I remember Sister Clare once told Julianne that she was as 'bold as brass'. I liked this phrase and used it to tease Julianne, though secretly I loved the image. Her boldness was one of the things I admired about her. She was brave, bright, shining. The way she jumped in at the deep end of any topic of conversation, eyes flashing.

As I talk to Michael tonight, I'm able to remember Julianne without fear of going over the falls into chaos. I've survived the memories of her that have returned, and Michael's question is an invitation that I want to accept. With him, it's safe to think about her.

Now, in the shadows of the day room, it's almost as if I can see her next to me, holding her head at an angle and looking into the distance, her eyes squinting in that familiar way as if she's searching for something. Then she looks directly at me, her eyes soften and relax, and she gives me her entire attention.

Returning her gaze, I'm able to comprehend the circumstances of her death with a clarity I've not experienced before. I can look her in the eye; I can see what happened. Face it. Survive in the face of it.

Words escape me, pouring out before I can think of what I'm saying. 'She died in a hospital in Sydney. They killed her because she spoke about secret things. They don't like you doing that. They zapped her mind with electricity until her heart gave out. They killed her. And she knew what they were doing.'

Michael's hand strays to his throat, and his thumb begins to stroke the small depression at its base. Except for this movement, he's quite still, facing me.

His presence is as reassuring as my own breath, drawing me to the place where all my confusions merge into the single thought of her.

'You're saying that Julianne died from ECT?' he asks.

'Yes, and from the drugs they were giving her.'

'So this wasn't you?'

'No. Julianne. Her, not me.'

'And this was in a psych hospital?'

'Yes, a psych hospital. We'd been at uni. Everything got too intense – the war, the Church, her father's death, everything – and she had a breakdown. They brought her here, to M Ward–'

'Here?' Michael is obviously taken aback.

'Yes, her bed was in the women's dorm. I visited her here.'

'You sure, Pauls?' Michael is looking at me strangely.

'Yes, that's what happened. She was here in M Ward, and then they took her to a hospital in Sydney. She died there. Her heart stopped beating. At midnight.' I pause and take a breath. It's important I get this right. 'The post-mortem report said the cause of her death was poisoning from an overdose of the drugs they gave her, but I think it was from ECT as well. I read a newspaper article about it.'

'That's just so...' Michael pauses. 'I don't know what to say. You both had breakdowns, ECT, the works. No wonder you've been confused.' He takes my hand. 'And you'd known each other since you were kids?'

'I always knew her,' I say.

The whole story spills out then, with no distinction between reality and delusion, between Julianne and me, between now and then. It comes in fits and starts at first, and then in an unstoppable flow of memories, tears and release. And as I become used to speaking of my past, I begin to feel less overwhelmed by the energy of the narrative. I find my self in the place where true words come from. I am what I say, and what I say has meaning. It brings me to life.

Michael listens in the way you always hope you'll be listened to when it matters. A rhythmic listening, an ear in the heart. His kindness makes me realise how lonely I've been since Julianne died.

***

Later, lying in bed and trying to sleep, I still feel overwhelmed by grief but now also by exhaustion. It's four years since Julianne died, and I think this is the first time I've cried over her loss.

During my first breakdown in 1968, I was in shock, disconnected from my loss and anguish. In this state of emotional paralysis, I didn't grieve Julianne – I *was* her. When my delusion fell away, she disappeared.

The ECT and antipsychotic drugs eradicated her from my life until my second breakdown, when the delusion returned. The feelings I did have, of dislocation, confusion, despair, didn't seem to be associated with anything I could name.

Now, Michael has helped me connect with the fact that Julianne is dead. He has come inside my inner world and shown me her death and my loss. I can now think about her, talk about her, remember her without breaking open. Eventually, I fall asleep.

When I wake up a few hours later, I sit in the dark on the easy chair beside the window, aware that I'm alone. Julianne is gone, and I am here without her.

A stream of memories takes me back to our first year at university. One day I was waiting for her in her room at Garran Hall when the door flew open. She was dancing around in her favourite yellow dress, waving a prescription for the contraceptive pill in the air and proclaiming that this was the beginning of a new era in her life.

We'd both been reading D.H. Lawrence, and I remember us sitting in the cafeteria talking about his poetry. Julianne said that his poem about the red geranium was her favourite. She was excited, telling me that she agreed with Lawrence that yearning is the most important precondition for creativity. She said, 'To be creative, you have to long to create something beautiful, something that hasn't existed before.'

I wonder what Michael would make of this idea; I must ask him tomorrow.

Tonight, memories of Julianne keep coming. I see us sitting at the desk in her Garran Hall room, analysing the Pope's encyclical on birth control. We try to apply the rules of logic that we're studying in our philosophy class but, in the end, we decide that logic isn't the issue. For us, famines and desperate poverty and mothers watching their children starve are the issues. I hear the precise inflections of Julianne's voice, see her smile as she turns to face me. It's the complicit smile of someone acknowledging that we have no other choice; we can no longer believe in the infallibility of the Pope. For us, this is a momentous realisation.

Julianne is present and as close as my breathing. I'm reminded of how she talked with her whole body. She almost danced when she solved a problem or reached a decision she'd been struggling with. Now she's here with me, and I can't stop crying. I never fully realised how much the emptiness in my life was due to her absence from it. And I never understood the impact of her father's death. In spite of our closeness, it remained a void: unapproachable, unspeakable.

Tonight, my grief is myself, experienced at last, spoken and acknowledged. It's where my breath goes to and comes from, the pain and the loss I've not allowed myself to feel. Telling Michael has been the turning point for me. That, and the closeness I feel now to Julianne. I begin to believe I can live.

***

In the following days, I'm still distracted by memories – of Julianne, of growing up, of our first year at university. I'm trying to piece it all together, see it as a whole rather than as fragments scattered through my mind like the aftermath of a catastrophe.

I remember clearly the day Julianne lost herself.

At lunchtime I was waiting for her in the Garran Hall dining room. As soon as I heard her voice, I knew something was wrong. I turned to the door and saw her waving a newspaper in the air and shouting about Vietnam. 'They're dropping bombs, napalm. They're killing children. It's criminal. We have to stop it,' she cried.

People stopped eating and turned towards her as she made her way between the tables, continuing her tirade about the war, the killings, the villages on fire.

I rushed to her, and when I put my arm around her, she collapsed against me, sobbing uncontrollably.

Once we were in her room, she sat on the bed, taking my hand in both of hers, pulling it towards her and shaking it. 'What's wrong?' she cried. 'What's wrong with me?' I had no idea what to do, what to say. I stared around the room as if an answer would magically appear from the bookshelves or walls.

Our first year at university had started out as a huge adventure. On the first day of term we'd sat in the cafeteria, excitedly thumbing through our new textbooks and talking about the subjects we were taking.

Now, in M Ward, it seems much longer than four years ago. So much has happened. We were eighteen and so naive.

In 1968, the world erupted into chaos. There was so much to take in, so many new ideas for us to integrate into our understanding of life. The Vietnam War intensified that year, and every night there were news reports of soldiers killed, villages burned to the ground, bombs dropped on civilians. In the United States, millions of people marched for civil rights or protesting the war. There was violence and mayhem, cars burning, people killed, cities on fire. Bobby Kennedy and Martin Luther King Jr. were assassinated. In France, wildcat strikes were held across the country and, for a while, the government of Charles de Gaulle was on the point of collapse.

Here in Australia, young men were being put in jail for refusing to register for national service, and anti-conscription groups were becoming more militant.

For Julianne and me, 1968 was an initiation into a disintegrating society. That year we lost our innocence. I would sit in the lounge room at home with my family, watching violent black-and-white images on the small television screen spark and disappear. My heart was filled with feelings I couldn't identify, couldn't give voice to. I didn't know how to manage the intensity of my responses to violence, war, injustice, racism. I was trying to understand it all – as if it made sense.

I was also questioning the roles that women were conditioned to play in society. I was introduced to the feminist ideas of Simone de Beauvoir through her memoirs, and to Betty Friedan's in *The Feminine Mystique.* I now noticed that the world reported in the news was one of men and their exploits: men in suits, men in military uniforms, men reporting on their lives. When women appeared, they seemed like dolls – men's pretty accessories. I imagined a different path for myself. I wasn't going to stay at home looking after children my whole life; I wanted to be involved in what was happening in the world.

One night I watched a television documentary about the hippies who were congregating in San Francisco and going to rock concerts, dancing wildly and smoking marijuana. They looked like revellers at a medieval-style carnival or a fancy-dress party, and I was fascinated. Sensational news stories in the Australian media described how these hippies were espousing the virtues of 'free love' and advocating the use of drugs. Stories appeared of drug-affected youths jumping out of high windows in the belief that they could fly and running naked through the streets claiming to have seen God. It all seemed like a wild, unnerving madness to me.

My home life was rooted in religious beliefs and rituals, and family routines. Sunday Mass was followed by a roast dinner or a barbecue on the banks of the Murrumbidgee. When we were younger, my siblings and I had knelt with Mum and Dad for the nightly ritual of the rosary, and on weekdays I'd ridden my bike through the breaking dawn to early Mass. In winter, there was ice on the puddles in the lanes, and my fingers on the handlebars were stiff, but I loved those early mornings, the Latin of the Mass, the mystery of Communion.

We'd been raised to believe unquestioningly in the authority of priests and nuns. When my mother had told the parish priest that I wanted to go to university, he had warned her I'd lose my faith if I studied philosophy. And he was right.

For months Julianne and I argued this way and that on Church doctrines and dogmas. In our philosophy class, we studied arguments for the existence of God and found them unconvincing. Eventually, we took our first breaths as atheists together. But while doubt had been an expansive experience, outright disbelief stripped us of all our certainties. God had held everything together: our sense of who we were, our families, our community and society. He had been the answer to all our questions.

In the end, I discovered there was not one prayer left in me. The doctrines and the rituals simply fell away. And once God ceased to exist, I lost the ground of my being. The universe seemed cold and impersonal; death cast a long shadow on my life. I didn't know where to look for truth and meaning. Life seemed random and absurd.

I was falling into the darkness, cut loose from nearly every bond except with Julianne. Our friendship was the one thing that made sense.

***

In the myth, the day Persephone was abducted into the underworld started out like any other. The sun shone brightly while Persephone and her friends played and collected flowers in the fields.

The day that Julianne went mad had also begun like any other. As usual, we'd planned to meet for lunch and then spend the afternoon studying together. Instead, Julianne was seized by a dangerous god and carried off. Life was never the same again. When she sat on her bed and asked, 'What's wrong with me?' I had no answers.

I suggested that we go home to her family, but she didn't want to worry them. So we spent the next two days and nights together at my family home, ensconced in my room. It was on the ground floor and had its own entrance from the garden, and it became our refuge as Julianne became more distraught. I had no idea what was happening. Once, when we went upstairs, she saw my mother doing the ironing. 'The trouble with you Keoghs is you're all too bloody normal,' she said as she walked through the dining room.

In my room, Julianne obsessed about the war. She wanted to give a speech to the old men in parliament who were sending boys off to fight. She wrote it down quickly, not pausing to think, covering page after page, begging the government to consider the suffering involved, urging them to listen to their hearts. I was overwhelmed and awed by the speed of her thoughts, and the wildness and intensity of her feelings. Her mind was a whirlwind, drawing everything into its orbit, including me.

In the eye of the storm of madness there's a kernel of sanity that's so clear and so true, you think you're in the presence of Truth distilled and laid bare.

My instinct was to protect her, keep people away. I could see how disturbed she was, but I kept thinking that she would soon recover, come back to herself, and I was caught up in our crazy conversations. We laughed until we cried about the absurdities of the world, about the Pope, about sex, about the Buddhist concept of 'no-mind'.

'My head's exploding,' Julianne told me. 'It's on fire.'

By Monday morning, my mother was aware that something was wrong and made an appointment for Julianne at the local doctor's clinic a few blocks away.

I gave her some of my clothes to wear. She was less talkative as we walked down to the clinic in the bright sunshine. 'Do you think he can help me?' she asked. I told her I was sure he could, and I tried to hide that I was worried. Coming out of my dark room into the light and the familiar streets, I saw that we'd crossed some line, though I couldn't think what it might be. Neither of us had had much sleep, and Julianne was clutching my arm so tightly it hurt. She'd put my jumper on back to front.

In the waiting room, one wall was covered in postcards from all over the world. I stood staring at them while Julianne was in with the doctor. My eyes registered the different scenes, the tropical beaches and the European cities, but I couldn't think. My mind was blank except for a buzzing headache, the sound of locusts gathering.

I remember what happened next as if the events are occurring now, in front of me.

I hear Julianne shouting. Minutes later, the doctor opens the door, takes a couple of strides out of his office and asks the receptionist to call an ambulance.

Julianne appears close behind him, her hair a mess, partly tied back and partly falling over her face, her eyes intense and bright. She's holding the bust of a woman's head high above her like a trophy. The logo of a well-known contraceptive pill is attached to its base, and I realise it has reminded Julianne of the Pope's ruling on birth control.

I take the bust out of her hands, place it on the desk and hug her. She puts her arms around me and her head on my shoulder. She begins to cry. I hear the doctor talking on the phone. 'Paranoid schizophrenia,' he says. 'Immediately.'

Everything takes place very fast, but stylised, not quite real, a movie scene that I'm watching from the front row. The ambulance pulls up at the door of the clinic, and two paramedics jump out. The doctor leans down to speak to one of them while the other puts his arms around Julianne's shoulders and guides her to the door.

It's clear that she doesn't want to go with him; she pulls away and stares at me, confused. Without hesitation, the paramedic turns her back towards the door and escorts her outside. I follow, hearing the ambulance doors slam shut, the motor revving. I stand there on the footpath, watching the ambulance disappear down Madigan Street.

I'm numb. They've taken her away. I've abandoned her. I walk home along the suburban street, registering nothing.

***

One rainy day in M Ward, Kate McNamara introduces me to a new way of thinking about the word 'mad'. We're sitting with Michael at one of the laminex tables in the day room, drinking coffee and talking about life on the ward.

'I don't think I'm ever going to get out of here,' says Kate.

'Yes, you will,' I say. 'You're unwell right now, but things will get better.' I'm aware that I sound exactly like my mother.

'Unwell! I'm not *unwell.* I'm mad. And so are you. You'd better get used to it.'

'Mad?' No one has ever said this to my face before. I feel as if I've been injected with a cardiac stimulant.

'Yes, mad, like the rest of us in here. Don't look so startled. We're all lunatics. That's why they've locked us up.'

'But we're not locked up,' I say. 'We're voluntary patients, and this is an unlocked ward.' Our conversation is making me anxious.

'So you voluntarily have ECT, do you?'

I'm confused. I've never thought about this before. 'I think I might have signed some papers,' I say. 'Yes, I think I did.'

'Christ, Pauls, that clinches it. You really are mad.'

'But we're not locked up in here.'

'Technically, you're right. We're not locked up, but we might as well be. Where else can we go?'

She has a point, one I'm well aware of. I look at her, and something shifts in me. Kate isn't afraid to say she's mad. She's defiant and forthright. Not ashamed, not humiliated. She doesn't hide herself away, or try to pretend everything's fine.

When I had my first breakdown, I was taken to a private psychiatric clinic located in a large old building on a hill in North Sydney. One of the other patients in my room used to steal my toilet bag and clothes. When I asked for them back, she would say, 'We're all God's mad creatures,' and walk off. I mulled over the idea that I might be mad, terrified by it. Being mad felt shameful and sinister, and I would never say the word out loud.

I've been diagnosed as 'schizophrenic', but that hasn't helped me at all; it means nothing to me. I'd hardly heard the word before Julianne's diagnosis. And the explanation that I have a chemical imbalance in my brain is confusing. The word 'schizophrenic' makes me feel cut apart, split open. It makes me feel that something incomprehensible is happening to me, whereas I can relate to the word 'mad' even if I find it deeply disturbing.

Schizophrenic, I belong to science; mad, I belong to the human race.

We all understand King Lear's confusion and despair. And Hamlet – his hallucinations tell us of his grief. Don Quixote's tale is a classic for a reason. We can relate to the madness in these stories and many others. All through history, there have been mad people who've seen things that aren't there, heard voices when no one is speaking, who've become strangers to their loved ones.

But I can't relate to the idea of schizophrenia, and I'm sure I'm not alone in this.

I've heard a saying that words are either like trees or like sores. Words that are like trees put roots deeply into the earth and reach high into the heavens. I don't know if the word 'mad' reaches into the heavens – though I suspect it did for Julianne – but it does reach into history and into our souls. It's part of the spectrum of human experience. It speaks to me and to people generally, mad or not, while the word 'schizophrenic' is like a sore, making me ill and cutting me off from other people.

Sitting here with Kate and Michael in the day room, I now see myself in a whole new way. Since my diagnosis I've felt humiliated, unworthy and degraded. But as Kate says, I have to get used to the idea that I'm one of 'them', the mad ones. I have to see that madness is something that could happen to anyone. I need to acknowledge the state I'm in, wholly admit to it.

Easy to say, harder to do, but I can at least begin to think more freely about my experiences, and those of Julianne, Michael, Kate and other patients in the ward. 'Mad' is a heavy word, but I think I can carry it. I already feel stronger.

***

For the first time since I've been a patient in M Ward, I go into the female dormitory for a reason other than ECT treatments. The last time I visited there was when Julianne was a patient four years ago. Kate and I have been talking about her favourite metaphysical poets, and she wants to show me a book of poems. As we walk into her room, I'm shocked by a flash of recognition. I look towards the corner next to a window.

There we are: Julianne and I sitting cross-legged on the bed. Julianne is telling me about a vision she had that revealed to her the connection between music and mathematics. She explains carefully that music is a series of interlinked mathematical problems and their solutions. She closes her eyes for a few seconds, enclosing this thought in the interior space of her being. Her voice is slow and deliberate, each word drawn up from somewhere deep inside her. She says that music is in our bodies, in the sky. In someone's scream. It's in a flower. In everything.

But then she pauses and looks directly at me, a flash of excitement in her eyes, her voice lit up. 'You know, the world's not like we thought. The world plays. It's music. We live in music, and it lives in us.'

As Kate and I walk out of the dormitory, it hits me. That visit to Julianne was the last time I saw her.

I'm overwhelmed by memories. I see Julianne as she was through thousands of our conversations, her familiar gestures matching the rise and fall of her precise and emphatic speech. I think of how she'd look when she was searching for the right word: she'd narrow her eyes and stare into the distance beyond my shoulder. She'd laugh and brush her hair back off her temples with both hands, then shake her head, letting her hair fall around her face again. She completed this little ritual with a self-conscious deliberation, adjusting her glasses and smiling her slightly myopic smile.

I think now that beneath all her confusion, Julianne saw the world as the mystics see it. She understood a profound truth that I reach for but can't quite grasp. In some essential region of herself, Julianne was whole and unbroken within the music.

4

Inside the Green Bell

he is white pain flowering
he touches me
we fly
laugh at the sky

Michael wants us to get engaged. There's an urgency about it for him, an enthusiasm for the wedding ceremony and for the idea of marriage that I find irresistible. It's simple and obvious: I love him, I can't imagine life without him, so we get a day pass from M Ward and go on a mission into Civic Centre to buy our engagement rings.

It's one of Canberra's archetypal spring days: cool blue sky and warm sunshine, with the hint of perfume from wattles in bloom along the road and plum trees pink with blossom. Michael and I hold hands and make jokes about being escapees, free at last. But in Civic Centre the streets are too close and too hectic. People hurry by, cars swerve around corners, loud music blasts from a record shop, and I feel exposed and uncertain. I can barely process the light, the noise, the rush, but we have rings to buy, so I take deep breaths.

As we cross Garema Place, we see a small market selling crafts and jewellery. Without hesitation, Michael steers us towards a colourful stall with handbags hanging above a table of silver jewellery. We're attracted by the rings with Celtic designs. Michael becomes excited as he tells me about the ancient *Book of Kells* in Dublin's Trinity College Library, the delicate knots and patterns painted on its pages.

'Look at this, Pauls,' he says, interrupting himself and holding a ring out for me to examine. 'It's the infinity symbol repeated in a circle.'

I take the ring and see that it's composed of two silver bands twining around each other. I think this symbol is perfect for us. Our love is about space: it's limitless.

'"Hold infinity in the palm of your hand,"' Michael quotes.

'Good ole William Blake knew a thing or two.'

I put on the ring – an exact fit.

Michael quickly tries on a few with the same design until he finds one that fits him. He gives it to me and insists that I take off the ring I've just put on. 'Let's exchange rings,' he says. I like the idea and hold out my hand. He slips my ring on the fourth finger of my left hand. I do the same with his, pushing it over his knuckle, my heart radiant. The moment the rings are on, Michael is kissing me.

The Spanish man behind the counter laughs. 'You'd better watch him,' he says. 'He's after your heart.'

As we walk away, arm in arm, I can't stop smiling.

Later, when we're eating toasted sandwiches at a cafe, Michael tells me more about Jumping Creek, the small property he owns near Candelo on the south coast of New South Wales. 'You'll love it, Pauls,' he says. 'The house is a bit dilapidated and neglected, but the countryside is really pretty. Rolling hills all around and a creek running through. It's just waiting there for us to fix up, make a home of it.'

'It sounds perfect,' I say. 'My dream house is small but has big windows, lots of light, wooden floors and stone walls.' I imagine living with Michael in this house. Flowers on the windowsills and a view from the kitchen sink: green hills, watercolour sky, drifting clouds. I hold this image in my mind and feel a sense of homecoming.

Michael raises his hand and smiles. 'I'll wave my wand–'

'And cosy,' I continue, laughing. 'Rugs and cushions thrown over the floors.'

'A den! It'll be our place. Let's have the wedding down there, invite all our friends. Make a festival of it, lots of people and music.'

'Vivaldi and Dylan. All our favourites.'

'Purcell and The Incredible String Band,' he says. 'We'll have the ceremony inside the birch spinney, then throw a huge party.'

Michael's hand is lying flat on the table, his new ring on his finger. I put my hand next to his, noting the contrast between them. One is the hand of a pianist, long and bony but strong, with fingernails that are short and ovoid. The other is pale and small, but looks capable and trustworthy with its square shape and blunt fingers. I can hardly believe it's mine. It feels separate from me, lying there like a porcelain sculpture, unreal next to Michael's tanned hand with its knotty veins and nicotine-stained fingers.

I like these different hands, and they like each other. All afternoon, as we negotiate shops and crowds, they seek each other out; they play together, showing off their silver finery. They are like the hands in that Escher sketch, bringing each other into being. Him drawing her drawing him.

We come across a fabric shop called George's and stand together at the front window, looking at a roll of cotton wrapped around a mannequin. I lean against Michael, and he puts his arm over my shoulder. The fabric has a vivid border, a swirling design of flowers and leaves, and we decide that it would make the perfect wedding dress.

Then, in the optometrist's where Michael is getting his glasses fixed, I catch sight of myself in a mirror. My mood sinks. I see an imposter, a girl in jeans playing at being normal. I smile at her while the noise in my head attacks me for thinking that Michael could possibly love me. I turn the ring around on my finger, but I have lost my lightness.

At a health food shop in an arcade, we do a serious sweep of the counters, making extravagant plans for macrobiotic diets and yoga retreats. But when I try to pay for a bag of almonds, I can't count out the right change, and my hand dipping into my purse is shaking too much to pick up the coins.

***

Back at the hospital, we show off our rings to the other patients and the nurses. 'We're getting hitched,' says Michael to the group gathered around us. 'A wedding, marriage, kids, the whole trip.'

I'm standing next to him, amazed at the picture he's painting, daring to believe that we can make it happen. Just weeks ago, I wanted to die. Now I'm planning an idyllic life in the countryside with the man I love.

'They're not proper engagement rings – you're supposed to have diamonds,' says ward prefect Lydia, pointing at my hand.

'Not for this engagement,' says Michael, smiling. 'See the Celtic infinity knot? Diamonds are old hat. Take it from me, these are official. Very cool.'

Michael is wearing his yellow and purple-striped beanie and a Nepalese waistcoat, and I've changed into my favourite dress of flowing cotton in a Native American print design. Hand in hand, we waft around the hospital corridors, oddly matched, strangely translucent. I'm in a state of shock, but this time it's the shock of happiness, the belief in a future with a man who, in spite of everything, loves me.

Later that night, Michael shows me a poem called 'Always a season' that he wrote as we sat together at a table in the day room. He tells me it's dedicated to me.

all is new
more than once
under the sun

see all
for the first time
or as
for the first time

'a time for peace
I pray
it's not too late'

and yes
there is for love
always a season.

***

During my teens and childhood, my imagination was inspired by archetypal figures. I was captivated by the various faces of the suffering Christ and by the lives of saints such as Francis of Assisi. I collected holy cards of bright winged angels and archangels. In high school, I was entranced by the love poetry of *The Song of Songs.* Later, I moved on to the vagabond, Bob Dylan, with his uninhibited sexuality, his poetic lyrics and his voice like broken marbles.

Michael fits the same archetype as Dylan – a kind of masculinity that I find exciting, a physicality that is fluid, ambiguous and roguish. He's a shy exhibitionist, sensitive and outrageous, old-fashioned and avant-garde, earnest and ironic. His manner of listening, his responsiveness to the lives of others, and his ability to be present to whatever is happening makes him many friends on the ward. But he also attracts critics – people either love him or hate him. He's vocal about his drug use and his lifestyle as a junkie and a hippie, and some people don't like this openness. It's a quality that's somehow both an expression of naivety and a deliberate baiting of prejudices.

Still, Michael speaks everyone's language on the ward, whether it's talk of drugs or depression, or patients just feeling hassled and out of it. He takes our despair and desperation, and turns it into poetry. For Michael, we're all 'prisoners of the Hotel Grand', a band of escapees from reality occupying a purgatorial space, belonging nowhere. The day room is the hotel lobby, our visitors emissaries from another world.

One of these emissaries is a family friend of mine, Father Peter Gannon, a young priest with a ruddy face and open smile. Michael likes him and enjoys his sense of humour. They sit together in the day room, laughing and telling jokes, while I lurk around, ungrateful and resentful. I believe that the priest is trying to get me to return to the faith; although, as Michael points out, he doesn't actually talk to me about religion.

After Father Gannon leaves the ward, Michael tells his jokes to the other patients and me. 'What do storks do on Sunday? Fly over the convent to scare the hell out of the nuns!' Our friends scream with laughter.

All of us in M Ward are troubled and self-absorbed, and Michael is no exception, but he has a way of sharing his world that gives the rest of us hope for another sort of existence. He's diffident and reticent at the same time as being attentive and focused. He carries about him an air of aloof attention, a stooping tallness that's both angular and graceful as he bends to listen more closely to the person he's talking to or as he leans forward in a chair to listen to music.

Into a bleak environment, Michael brings soul – the dreaming, imagining part of ourselves, a sense of the essence of things, the inner life.

***

The sign *Nil by Mouth* is hanging on the door of my room. It means I'll be having ECT tomorrow – the first of another series of treatments. I'll be having it every second day for a week or more. I'm angry. I flick the sign with my hand as I walk past, and it falls to the floor.

'Nil by Mouth,' says Michael in a lilting accent as he picks it up. 'Sounds like a Welsh railway station.'

'Yeah, well, I don't think any trains are coming tonight. We're stuck here.'

He hangs the sign back on its hook, and we settle into my room.

'No trains scheduled, perhaps,' he says, 'but it's the unscheduled ones that have the most interesting destinations.' He stretches back into the chair by the window and places his hands behind his head. 'So, where would you like to go?'

'Anywhere away from here.'

'Let's make it St Petersburg, or Tierra del Fuego – or, for something completely different, how about ... Gundagai?'

'Gundagai?'

I laugh, but my stomach is tight with fear. The night before ECT is always terrifying; each time, it feels like the last night of my life. I dread the fasting, the thirst and the waiting, the machine behind my head, the doctor and a nurse at my side, and the anaesthetic dragging me into unconsciousness.

Julianne seems very near to me as I think of what's ahead. Her presence hovers so close, I don't know if I'm clinging to her or she to me. What I do know is that I have to resist falling into her death again.

Michael is reading my book of Japanese poems, and I'm going through the contents of my drawers, obsessively folding and refolding my clothes and putting them in piles on my bed. I imagine the dormitory set up for ECT treatments, and it takes on a strange, nightmarish quality. I think of myself lying with my head at the wrong end of the bed, listening to the machine as it's wheeled closer. The doctor in his white coat is hovering over me like a ghost, fiddling with the dials, checking his watch. The fear in these imaginings sucks the air out of my lungs.

***

I'm starting to stir, don't know where I am. The room comes and goes. Vision is blurred. I'm thick with drugs, body heavy and unresponsive. Brain is stunned and burnt. Can't work out where I am. Who I am. What's happening.

I become aware of sounds, a voice close by that seems to be chanting a prayer. As I drift, its rhythm is a focus, something familiar that draws me upwards. I'm trying to open my eyes, then closing them against the sliding geometry of the room. The voice fades, and I fall away. My brain is sore.

Sometime later, the voice starts again. As I focus on the pitch and rhythm, someone takes my hand. I can't find his name, but I'm aware that he's someone I love. Someone who gives me a clearer sense of myself. Someone who strokes my hand.

I lie there listening to his voice as it flows over me. His words start to make sense: he's playing a game. He's asking me if I'm Helen of Troy, waiting for Paris to return. Or Lilith, goddess of the night. He suggests that maybe I'm Anna Karenina, or possibly Marianne from the fish'n'chip shop. Then he bends down and whispers in my ear, telling me I'm Pauls, his beloved. 'You've had ECT. You're dopey from the anaesthetic.'

I begin to remember. I'm aware that he's Michael, and I know who I am. Through the fog, I find my way to him. I am his beloved. I turn over in the bed and fall asleep.

After that, Michael always sits next to my bed while I sleep after shock treatment. It's impossible not to love someone who sits by you as you sleep. It's a most delicate, most profound intimacy.

***

One evening after dinner, my parents arrive in the day room, my mother carrying a small bunch of sweet peas, my father dressed in a suit and tie. It's been a while, and I've been looking forward to them coming – I want to tell them my big news. I bring them to the table where Michael and I have been sitting, and I introduce him to them.

As soon as we sit down, I extend my hand to show them the ring. 'Michael and I are engaged.' My mother looks at it, then at Michael and me, confused and alarmed. This is the first time my parents have met him. This is not how things are done.

'We didn't want diamonds,' I say. 'This is an infinity engagement ring. Michael has one too.'

'You're ... engaged?' Mum says, clearly disturbed.

For what seems like a long time, no one says anything.

Then Michael says, 'Yes. We love each other and we're going to get married.'

'There's no need to rush this,' Dad says, pulling himself up on his chair.

'What do you mean? Aren't you happy for me?' My voice rises above the hum of conversation in the room. People stop talking and look in our direction.

My father takes my mother's hand to steady himself. It's important not to make a scene. 'Of course we're happy for you,' says Mum, though it's quite obvious that they're not. Her tone is that of someone placating a child.

'This is not something we need to talk about right now,' says Dad. 'We'll have lots of time to discuss this when you're well again.'

'Michael and I are getting married as soon as we get out of here and find a place to live,' I say, determined that we settle this now.

'You aren't well at the moment,' Dad says carefully. 'I think you should wait a while before you make a decision like this. At least six months.'

Silence descends on the table again. I feel the weight of their opposition, and I'm suddenly unable to stand up against them.

Michael turns towards me and takes my hand. 'Perhaps we could wait three months,' he says. 'What do you think, Pauls?'

'Okay,' I say, relieved that the tension has been diffused.

The conversation immediately turns to other topics. Before long, Mum and Dad are leaving, the small posy of sweet peas still lying on the table. I want to throw it in the bin. I don't want sweet peas; I want them to be happy for me. I'm angry with myself for needing their approval, angry that I'm 'unwell', frustrated that everything is so complicated. I pick up the posy, take it to the laundry and put it in a vase, feeling trapped.

***

One day when we're in the green bell, Michael tells me the story of Lancelot and Guinevere. It's overcast outside the bell, and shady and warm inside. As he talks, Michael is massaging my forehead and pressing down on the base of my skull. I relax easily into his tales of Camelot. According to the legend, Michael tells me, Queen Guinevere is condemned by King Arthur to burn at the stake for her infidelity, but at the last minute Lancelot sweeps in and saves her from the pyre.

Michael kisses my neck and claims that he is my Lancelot and I am his Guinevere. He plans to save me from M Ward and make a life for us at Jumping Creek. We're hopeless romantics, children playing dress-ups, but I enjoy the illusion. I'm happy to borrow some of Guinevere's glamour, and I'm charmed by the idea of Michael as a twentieth-century knight, riding courageously through the taboo regions of our culture, writing poems about his journeys and then sweeping me off to a rural retreat. I'm his beloved, captivated by the dream of love.

Later, alone in my room, I begin to imagine what marriage with Michael will be like in a practical sense.

Being a romantic doesn't seem compatible with my feminism. As I see it, Simone de Beauvoir and Jean-Paul Sartre are the ideal couple – but they never married. When Julianne and I read de Beauvoir's *Memoirs of a Dutiful Daughter,* she became my hero. She wanted to be a writer and a philosopher, and she refused to marry Sartre even though he proposed several times. She believed marriage would prevent them from having the equal relationship that she wanted, and I agreed with her.

But now I'm beginning to think that a different kind of relationship is possible.

I've just turned twenty-three, and I want to be a feminist *and* a romantic. I decide that Germaine Greer is wrong in her critique of romantic love: that it's an egoistic, lustful, masochistic, sentimental fantasy. I prefer to go with Shulamith Firestone's view that love is only destructive in the context of inequality. I can't imagine Michael wanting to be in a position of power over anyone.

For Michael, it's important that the life we live is true and real. When I talk about de Beauvoir's objections to marriage, he says, 'There'll be no hubby and wifey stuff with us. We'll be real – really you, really me. No acting out roles, laying down rules.' I agree, and I'm pinning all my hopes on us blazing a trail into unpredictable territory.

I don't see, around me, any examples of the sort of marriage I want. My parents have a strong bond and it's obvious they love each other, but they don't seem to have an equal partnership. Their marriage works because of strict gender roles: my mother's domain is the home; my father's is the outside world. I don't want to be confined to domesticity, and I want the right to have opinions on politics and world events.

I wonder what a true partnership would be like. I've never seen one, but I'm determined that there will be no strict gender roles and obligations in my marriage to Michael. Ours will be a journey into a new and creative way of being together.

***

We pass the days in our usual hangouts – my room, the day room, the hospital cafeteria and the green bell – sharing memories and fantasies, delusions and self-deceptions, and finding happiness in our strange fit with each other. But it's a broken wholeness: love in a time of madness, a blind and wild joy rampaging through bodies mired in grief. For long moments, the mind is quiet, just a witness, startled and wondering.

Other times, it ruminates and probes, and Michael is often the focus of these ponderings. He perplexes me. He's the kind of puzzle you can't solve, because it doesn't conform to any familiar principles. He's a shapeshifter, a chameleon. While he resembles the representations of Christ that filled my imagination throughout my childhood, and fits my idea of the vagabond, he could also be a revolutionary from Trotsky's day. He's an adventurous, chivalrous knight, but he's also a social critic, very much of these times.

His energy and motivations are deeply rooted in his inner world. He has a mercurial style and a way with language, creating imaginary worlds or recalling them from legends, spinning stories on short walks to the hospital cafeteria or while waiting for doctor's appointments. He's volatile, one minute animated and enthusiastic, the next moody and introverted. I find these transformations exciting, mystifying.

Love has drawn my entire life's dreaming together in one sleight of hand and transferred it to Michael. He's highly creative, compassionate, funny, attentive. Being with him is a dynamic play of feeling, music, imagining and storytelling. My ego is shattered. I find it hard to make decisions, to think rationally. For me, our shared self fills this vacuum. As Michael's beloved, I have an identity to inhabit, one that takes me right out of my small and limited existence, placing me in the myth of romantic love.

***

Michael tells me that he's having a hard time getting his current book, *Memoirs of a Velvet Urinal,* published. He says that people just can't cope with his work.

Then he tells me that he's bisexual, and that some of the poems in *Memoirs* are about his sexual relationships with men. Although I'm surprised at first, it makes sense. Michael has a fluid sensuality and an androgynous personality, a blend of the masculine and feminine that complements his fine, angular body. I've never known a man like him before, and I haven't known anyone who's openly homosexual or bisexual.

Growing up in the Church, I formed the idea that sex between unmarried people was sinful, a lustful act, while 'conjugal love' between a married couple was holy and pure. But since losing my faith, I've rejected these ideas. For me, sex between consenting adults involves a natural pleasure that people should be free to engage in as they wish, whether they're homosexual, heterosexual or bisexual. The only hitch for me is that I can't bear to share a sexual partner with someone else.

Michael makes bisexuality seem an obvious way of being. He speaks of how easy it is to love both men and women, and says it would feel unnatural to be limited to having sex with only one gender. He feels that he's a third sex, both male and female, or either, depending on who he's with or what's happening.

I envy his ability to talk so unselfconsciously. I can engage in sex with pleasure and without inhibition, but I can't talk about it. There's some deep disconnect in me between language and the life of the body. My mind refuses any speech relating to body parts, functions, pleasures; it's all forbidden, off limits, except as an abstraction. I feel as though that part of my brain is actually missing.

The more Michael talks about his sexuality, the more I realise how little I understand of his life. I've read about homosexual literary figures like Oscar Wilde, and I know that sexual acts between men are still illegal in most of Australia, but I don't know what the personal costs might be for someone like Michael speaking and writing so openly. What I do know is that his sexuality means ostracism, bigotry, danger. I've read of 'poofter bashings', and of a man being pushed into the Torrens River and drowned for being homosexual. It was claimed that police were responsible.

I know Michael in my soul while at the same time I don't know him at all. I like this sense that he exists beyond my understanding and somehow beyond this life, in the world of his poetry where there are no limitations and no rules.

Alone and sleepless in my bed, I realise that while Michael is still something of a mystery to me, I don't really know who I am either. I'm questioning everything, and I can't find a place anywhere. Michael, at least, identifies with a range of subcultures: hippies, junkies, the poetry scene. He looks and acts as if he's on the side of the revolution; he describes himself as a 'freak' and derides 'straight' society. But while people might assume I'm a hippie because I have long hair and wear jeans, and sometimes long dresses, I don't think of myself as one. I don't think of myself as part of any group – even though, like Michael, I'm alienated by our materialistic society.

We're both outsiders committed to finding new ways of living and being, and there are no clear-cut lines for us. We're emotionally tied to some conservative values and opposed to others. Michael is a bit of a wheeler and dealer, at least as he describes it; he has bought and sold properties despite being a strong critic of capitalism. He wants to be a revolutionary poet but also supported by the established poetry scene. And he'd like us to get married. He says that he wants nothing to do with 'straight' society, but he craves acceptance and acknowledgement.

I'm caught in my own confusion of affiliations and values. One minute I'm an atheist, the next an agnostic, the next praying desperately to God for help. On some days I'm a feminist strictly opposed to patriarchal values, while on others I find myself dreaming of a wedding dress and a bouquet. I'm intellectually attempting to work it all out while emotionally unable to connect with a sense of self.

Our contradictions are woven through the stories we tell each other of our lives. M Ward is a place of storytelling as much as it's a space of gloom, extreme moods and empty routines, and our tales are healing. They weave our lives together in the face of a madness that threatens to tear everything apart.

***

One evening when the day room is full of patients and visitors, Michael tells me that he's made a deal with Sally, a nurse who often does night shift. If we're careful and are back before ten, we can slip outside for a while. Sally has henna-red hair and a bright, bantering energy that lightens the mood on the ward.

She gets on better with the patients than with the other staff, and she's turned a blind eye to night absences before. Grateful for the reprieve from the crowded day room, Michael and I take off to the lake shore.

It's dark inside the green bell, and the night air is cold. We wrap ourselves in Michael's coat for warmth and lean against the tree trunk. I hear water rats rummaging among the reeds, and through the willow branches I see the flickering lights of the city across the water.

The night is still and silent, and our voices are soft so as not to break the spell of our closeness, our warmth. Here in the green bell, intimacy is as easy as breathing.

Michael talks about our wedding and our life at Jumping Creek, describing the music filling the house, the cottage garden we'll create, and the friends dropping in to visit. We tease each other about our plans and laugh at the audacity of our hopes for a 'normal' life.

I roll us cigarettes and, not wanting to pollute the earth, Michael collects our butts and saves them in my empty Drum tobacco pouch. With Michael's arm around me, happiness and tenderness rise within me like waves from a deep ocean. I feel an ecstatic sense that the world is alive, that I'm alive.

I turn towards Michael as his face appears in the flash of a lit match, its planes and hollows exaggerated by the upward tilt of the flame. He seems suddenly a stranger, haunted and old. As he inhales on his cigarette, his eyes gleam with an otherworldly fire, some fierce and ageless wizardry.

I glimpse the vast and unknowable nature of his being, a spark of the eternal in him, and feel the shock of his otherness, his otherworldliness. I'm spooked, jolted out of our shared mood.

Michael senses my withdrawal and makes a joke, and, as we laugh, I see him again as his familiar self. But I know I have seen something in Michael, something distant and ancient, and it's eerie and unsettling, and thrilling.

Soon I'm aware only of Michael's presence, the soft air around us, and the damp, loamy smell inside the green bell. As I place my warm hand on his cool cheek, he presses his face into my palm and smiles. I know I'll never forget the way he looks at me, never be this happy again.

Sorcerer, note how the stars attend our banquet
And all the trees dance to our song
We drink yet our cup is overflowing
Ah truly, what have you done?

See in the water the long willow drifting
Time is an anchor and love's set us free
The lake is the sky and creation's exploding

In your eyes; come, dance with me.

We're sailing off in a ship of fools
Let heaven take care of the way
From here there is no place we've need of to go
Blind lovers, we've looked on the sun.

5

Life as a Poem

It's a sunny morning and light fills the day room. Kitchen staff are busy collecting our used breakfast plates and cutlery, stacking them on trolleys, their movements quick and deliberate. A small group of patients are talking at a table over coffees; others have taken solitary places on couches and chairs under the windows. Michael and I turn our backs to the room, sit on the floor in the corner facing the stereo cabinet, and listen to Chopin – nocturnes, waltzes, mazurkas; some melancholy and interior, others a dance of grace and joy, a play of sound that whirls around us. We imagine living in the city of music, nineteenth-century Vienna, attending concerts and balls in the palaces, wearing glorious clothes, fluttering our fans.

When another waltz begins, Michael turns up the volume, stands and, with a bow, takes my hand. The next minute we're dancing around the tables in a giddy release while someone claps and the Man from Kosciuszko waves his arms as if conducting an orchestra.

Before long a nurse appears and turns the music down, then frowns and sweeps out of the room. As we go back to our place on the floor, Michael is overtaken by a coughing fit – a harsh ripping of his chest that takes every bit of his attention. When it finishes, he narrows his eyes in exaggerated frustration and turns the music up again, very loud. For a few defiant moments it fills the space around us. Then, as he turns it down, he smiles and shrugs.

We get an ashtray from a table and light cigarettes. Michael blows smoke rings for my amusement, and they drift on the air between us. When he finishes his cigarette, he leans forward and moves into a rave about the music of Erik Satie. He says that all poems are songs, and poets wandering minstrels. I see the dream he's in and enter it without hesitation.

Michael's raves come in bits and pieces, so I can hardly put them together, hardly take it all in. Highs and lows, loves and hates, narratives of flight and coming down. Light seems to flicker through his being in shifting patterns as his mind entertains the many contradictions in his life and the world around him. With his thin body, long arms and strong hands, and his small, delicate head, Michael moves as though he's not quite at home on the earth. He's acutely sensitive to touch, to voice and sound, to ambience. He wears his soul as a skin, his only skin.

I write in my notebook, *Here in a nuthouse, crazy about you,* and hand it to him. 'Dig it,' he says, and we laugh – at ourselves, at the absurdity of everything. We make more plans for what we'll do when we get out. A long walk through the forests down the south coast. A journey by boat to Vienna and Greece. A future together.

***

'You know, religions are amazing fantasies,' says Michael later that day, as we walk towards the general hospital cafeteria.

'What do you mean?' I say.

'Well, religions are fantastic stories.'

I think about this for a minute. 'You can't say that religions are just stories. Every religion claims that its beliefs are the truth.'

'They do,' Michael says, turning towards me, 'but *my* religion says they're all stories and they're all true.' His eyes are shining.

'So who's your God, then?' I ask, puzzled. I think that Michael's family is Presbyterian – and he went to Sydney Grammar, an Anglican school – but in all our discussions my sense was that he didn't believe in any religion.

He answers, 'All of them, all the gods. I bow to Yahweh, Shiva, Allah, Jesus, Buddha–'

'Buddha's not a god.'

'He's a god to me – and so are Zeus, Apollo, Dionysus.'

'Then so are Hera and Aphrodite.'

'Definitely! They all come from the imagination,' he says, 'and that's what I worship – the imagination. And I serve them all. All the gods, all the goddesses.'

'That'd be chaotic. You'd never know where you are.'

'Do I look like someone who wants to know where he is?' he says, grinning.

'Well, you'd at least want to know what is true,' I say. I'd like to be clear on this.

'All the invisibles are true. There's no such thing as a false fantasy.'

'But fantasies are, by definition, *not* true.'

'Not real, maybe,' he says.

We walk in silence for a few moments. This is a lot for me to take in. Although I've lost faith in the God of Catholicism, I still carry a reverence for truth, and believe that truth and fantasy are opposites. Michael's ideas run counter to almost everything I've previously understood. I'm holding out for the experience of revealed truth, something I can believe without doubt. I'm no longer an atheist, but I'm not sure if I am an agnostic either. Maybe God is the intelligence of the universe, the designing force inherent in everything. A sublime energy. The earth itself, the night sky, the stars and the galaxies, spiralling infinity. 'God' seems like another word for the whole of creation. But that doesn't really get me anywhere. I still don't understand how it all holds together.

'What about the sacred in your scheme of things?' I ask Michael.

'Hmm. I reckon it's when the gods visit. Like now–' He pulls me towards him and kisses me.

In the cafeteria, we start speculating about black holes. I'm fascinated by them and want to understand how they're created, even though I haven't even the most basic grasp of physics. 'The problem with you is that you want to understand everything,' says Michael. 'I just want to feel okay. I think we're both screwed.'

He's right that my craving for answers is a problem. Once you've been mad, you can never again take the realm of the real as the only truth. I'm no longer content with bare reality. It's never 'what you see is what you get'; there's always something beyond appearances. But I can't pin down the idea of God, just as I can't explain Michael. They're mysteries. Everything is. And my brain can't accept this. It can't understand that there are no final answers to my questions.

***

For Michael, poetry is life itself. Living life as a poem is the true purpose of existence. He tries to view each event and every object through the eyes of his imagination. He has a way of being in the world that's open and spontaneous, a willingness to throw himself into whatever's happening and see through to its essence, its truth. There's never a sense of him being only half there.

When he was nineteen, Michael wrote in his diary: 'poetry is the blood in my veins, my mind, what I drink and who I kiss and who most I fear. It is me.' He seems to feel that poems are written through him, that in the act of writing poetry he becomes an instrument of a greater power. Sometimes he thinks of this power as a living poetic tradition, at others as the gods to which, in his unique way, he surrenders with passion, with devotion.

I've been writing poems since I was fourteen, but I haven't shared them with anyone – even Julianne, though she knew I wrote poetry. Now, tentatively at first, and then with more confidence, I give them to Michael to read, grateful that he takes them seriously as poems and as personal communications. He probes me with questions: 'What does this feel like? What does it make you think of?' After reading one of my poems, he says, 'With the first line, you stick the knife in. In the last line, you turn it.'

He gives me copies of his books *Streets of the Long Voyage* and *The Inspector of Tides,* both inscribed with loving dedications. He tells me that his third book, *Drug Poems,* was released at the beginning of the year, but he hasn't a copy on him to give me.

I start by reading his poem 'Letter to people about pelicans', and one afternoon when we're in my room listening to music, I tell Michael that I like its passion and irony, its absurdist humour. He says, 'What's a poem when we're all dying, the earth's dying, the animals are dying?' In the diffuse sunlight, we talk about a future where cities have become like the Warsaw ghetto, overcrowded and unbearably bleak.

Michael points to the silver Star of David he's wearing around his neck. 'I'm a Jew,' he says. 'We both are.' The truth in what he says has nothing to do with ancestry. With the Holocaust just a generation behind us, Jews constellate persecution and suffering on an archetypal level. Michael feels that he's one of the chosen – and one of the cursed. And he thinks I am too.

***

We're bent over coffees at a day-room table when a man walks up to us, takes a chair and begins talking. He has unruly dark hair and a beard, and he speaks to me as if he knows me. I'm polite to him, but it's only when he introduces himself to Michael as 'Ross' that my memories of him begin to surface.

I met Ross at a house party a couple of years ago. He was in the kitchen opening a bottle of beer with his teeth while looking sideways at me standing in the doorway. He and his two friends had a loutish energy about them, telling jokes and handing out drinks to anyone passing through. We got talking. He drove me home that night in his old green Riley with running boards down the sides and deep leather seats. We kissed in the car park of the Mount Ainslie lookout, listening to the Rolling Stones. In the next couple of weeks we saw each other a few times, but then Ross left for Sydney and I hadn't seen him since.

I study him as he and Michael make small talk. He's changed entirely; no wonder I didn't recognise him. His hair used to be shorter, and he was clean-shaven. And he had an easy smile that seems to have disappeared entirely. In its place is shocked confusion, as if someone has just shut a door in his face. Or as if he's forgotten who he is – or doesn't care to know.

'Yeah, got conscripted,' he says to Michael. 'Got the dummy's ticket in the birthday lottery. Was over there way too long.'

'Shit, man. What rotten luck. I got one too, but didn't pass the medical.'

'Yeah, well, them's the breaks,' Ross says, looking away.

'What are you doing here in M Ward?' I ask, aware of some tension in the air.

'I'm supposed to come every day. It's a joke. They're trying to get me to hate booze. Aversion therapy.'

'That's heavy, man,' says Michael. 'Are you into that?'

'It's complicated. Had a run-in with the law.' Ross's eyes drift off to the side again. I see no trace of the vintage car enthusiast whose heroes were James Dean and John Lennon.

'Oh, right,' says Michael. 'But the aversion therapy, is it working?'

'For them or for me?' Ross says grimly, pulling on his shirtsleeves.

We talk about M Ward then, the staff and the food. We don't talk about the war, and we don't ask Ross about his experiences as a veteran. It doesn't feel right.

When I met him, Ross was opposed to the war, and I'm confused and disturbed to think of him in Vietnam. I imagine him walking with his pack and his rifle along a jungle track while bombs explode around him and villagers run ahead of the fire. I hear helicopters shattering the sky and see thick smoke rising into the air. It comes to me that Ross may have killed people, and I feel sick, as though I've broken some taboo in having that thought. I wonder how Ross feels about it all.

After he leaves M Ward that day, I'm still having visions of his war experiences. It's one thing to imagine what war must be like; it's quite another to think of someone you know in the thick of it. I bring up war with Michael, talking about Ross while also trying to understand the hallucinations of battlefields, broken bodies and death that I had when I first came to the ward.

Growing up, I heard only a few anecdotes of my maternal grandfather's experiences in World War I, but I imagined many more. Pop lost his leg in Delville Wood near Pozières on the Somme in 1916, and as a small child I was fascinated by his stump and the fate of his missing limb. When my parents took us on visits to the Australian War Memorial, the constructed battle scenes inspired my visions of Pop fighting 'Ole Fritz'.

Forty-six thousand Australians lost their lives on the muddy battlefields of the Western Front. Pop's leg may have been the price he paid for his survival. His wound had been small to begin with, but as time passed with no medical help, gangrene set in. His leg was amputated at Rouen; in his diary, he wrote that he was living on a diet of champagne for a few days after the operation – presumably due to the lack of anaesthetics.

My paternal grandfather also fought in France, but I know even less about his involvement, and he died when I was two. A large sepia photo of him in his army uniform hung above the dining-room table at my grandmother's house, and I remember his dreamy expression, a soldier in a slouch hat watching over us like a guardian angel as we sat around the table drawing and playing with plasticine.

During my first days in M Ward, I found myself living through Pop's experiences, stuck in the trenches up to my thighs in freezing mud, watching gangrene fester in my dirty leg wound. Sometimes, I still feel that it's me in the trenches – that I'm him or he's me, I can't tell which. I feel the rot and the damp and the pain. The noise of gunfire and explosions, the lonely cries of men dying in the fields. I smell death and decay and blood. His trauma is my inheritance.

My fantasies of my grandfather's war merge with those of Vietnam and affect all of my responses to violence. I can't understand how, given poetry, music, art and the power of love, we still kill one another in the most horrific ways. It's yet another problem my mind obsesses over as if it could be solved, if only I could think of the solution.

When I talk this through with Michael, he tells me that there would be no war if we saw it through our imaginations. The earth wouldn't be destroyed by pollution and greed; no one would adhere to the perverted values of capitalist society. If we could see through the lens of poetry and love – if we saw truly with the imagination – we wouldn't destroy one another and the world we've been given.

As I mull over these ideas, the concept of truth changes for me. Although I've always loved music and poetry, before this breakdown I took an intellectual approach to life. I thought that truth was an abstract and objective quality. Now I think that it's multifaceted, multidimensional. It's bound up with facts but it goes beyond them. Truth is to be found in the exploration of the factual – in the relationship between facts, and between us and them. The truth of my grandfather's experience of war is to be discovered and revealed through an imaginative engagement with the physical details of the suffering he endured. Truth appears when matter and spirit merge. It's the human, subjective dimension of the factual. It's this I want to see through to and speak of, as best I can. If I can.

***

Early one evening, Father Gannon appears in the hospital cafeteria, looking for Michael and me. He places a plate of cupcakes covered in pink icing on the table and sits down.

'From a parishioner,' he says, offering me one. 'How've you been?'

'I'm good, thanks,' I say, smiling. I'm starting to like this man.

He turns to Michael. 'What about you?'

'Been better,' he says. 'Feel a bit hollowed out today. Got any jokes?'

'One I think you'll like,' Father Gannon says, winking at me. He pauses and sits back in his chair for effect. 'Why did the hippies go to Mass on the first day of Lent?'

Michael groans. 'This doesn't have anything to do with penance, does it?'

'No, not even close. Give up?' He takes our silence as our assent. 'Because they thought it was Hash Wednesday!'

Michael laughs and gently punches Father Gannon on the arm. 'You've got my number,' he says.

'I saved that one for you.'

I leave the table and line up to get another coffee for us, leaving Michael and Father Gannon talking. When I come back and give them their drinks, they're deep in conversation.

'I don't read much poetry, but your poems ... they're very good. There's a lot of love in them,' says Father Gannon.

'Yeah, poetry is love,' says Michael. 'It's the closest I come to praying. It's what I live for. That's what the two of us have in common – we live for our religions.'

'And from reading your poems, I'd say there are things our religions have in common too.'

'Well, yeah, you're right. Priest and poet, both of us voices crying in the wilderness.'

Although I'm curious, I leave them to their conversation. I feel that this is their private discussion.

I give them two of the cupcakes and bring the rest of the plate back to the ward to share around.

***

I've mostly come through the extremity of the psychosis that brought me into M Ward, but I exist in a permeable space, vulnerable to mad thoughts and wanderings. I've been trying to imagine that I'm not mad, that my mind isn't loud with noise, that my heart isn't pulled this way and that by joy, by pain; that it isn't pounded by memories and self-doubt. But I can't put together what sanity might feel like.

I'm often unreal to myself. Ordinary interactions can seem like hallucinations. I sometimes look at a commonplace object and can't work out what it is or what it's used for. The shapes and patterns in pictures can be unrecognisable and threatening. Everyday words like 'frog' or 'underneath' can take on sinister meanings.

Such states of mind are eased by Michael's presence. His voice is always associated with a feeling of clarity at the core of myself. 'What's happening?' he asks, seeing that I'm disoriented. I find it helpful to put my confusion into words, and Michael accepts the reality of the unreal, normalising it. He is Eros, leaning down to me, his arm around my shoulders, his lips on my cheek, on my ear. The golden-winged god, hovering, close. I'm brought back from the underworld into his presence and into the green bell.

Since I've met him, my experience of time has changed. I sense it unfurling as slowly as the frond of a tree fern. Moments expand into what the two of us call 'round time' – the boundless space inside the green bell. A feeling of infinity. Linear time is the clock ticking, counting the hours on the ward in regular beats, but there's no measurement for round time. It's a bird, free of its cage, flying into open sky. Our love has the quality of a lucid dream in which everything is connected. We discover the stillness in the dance and are absolved of doubt.

Saints tell us that love is at the heart of mysticism. With Michael, I discover mysticism at the heart of love.

For a long time after I lost my faith, I was nostalgic for a mythic world of mysteries and visions, in spite of the inner torment I suffered from the dark side of 1950s Catholicism. Nothing remained of the religion that had once sustained me. Now, with Michael, I'm rediscovering the stories of Jesus, the saints and angels, and connecting again with the breakaway life of the spirit.

In his poem 'Esaias', Michael describes the voice of a prophet, one voice in a vast multitude: 'and all his words are poems and his truths philosophies'. When we speak of Jesus, Michael refers to him as 'the Lord'. I see Jesus now as a man, not as a god. He was a charismatic revolutionary, a spiritual genius, storming into the temple and knocking over the tables of the moneylenders, furious that they were using a holy place to do business. He defied convention to befriend Mary Magdalene, and perhaps he did bring Lazarus back from a kind of death.

With Michael, I exist within a reality that my former rational, everyday self would have rejected as fantasy. I'm in touch with a state of being that transcends the world of appearances and opens me to love, to visits by gods and angels, and to miracles, poetry, music.

I'm no longer the rationalist, the atheist, the sceptic. Michael – and madness – have opened my eyes to invisible realities. I believe in the inner world of spirit and imagination. I feel that I belong here, with him – and that one day, the noise and the pain will pass, and there will just be the love.

***

Slowly focusing and refocusing my eyes, resting them between lines, I read through Michael's first two books, and poem after poem comes to life. Images emerge in rhythms and patterns, sometimes harmonious, sometimes dissonant, but always creating fully imagined worlds that invite me in.

I have little sense of personal boundaries; the distinction between myself and others is blurred. I don't always know whether my thoughts and feelings are my own, or if I'm accessing the inner worlds of other people. As I read, the experiences that Michael speaks of in his poems, the people and the landscapes that he describes, become more real to me than the life I've been living. I have an affinity with the visions of his poems. I belong with them, while the streets of Canberra and rooms of M Ward seem brittle and empty.

The qualities of Michael, the person I know, merge with the personae of his poems. The Michael I have fallen in love with is 'the inspector of tides' going for a walk 'dressed in clouds & with the wind & with some friends'. He is the minstrel who sang for his supper and slept in 'haysheds and corners out of the wind, wrapped in a wagga rug'. He is the Duke of Courland's son, living in a loft over the coach-house at the old Courland Penders family estate, feeling old, writing poems that are 'archaic'. In my mind, I'm there too, living with him, watching the flames of the fire 'rise and fall like waves', regretting nothing.

The Michael who says he loves me and wants to share his life with me is also 'the hermit of green light', living a solitary life in the woods tending broken birds, listening to the sound of the river and the 'imperfect silence', and finding, often, that 'it is enough'.

I have fallen in love with Michael, but also with his imagined selves, his imagined worlds. I enter his dreams and find they are mine: 'dreams of a perfect poem, something/which in the end requires no work. a swan, for example,/or a red, mossy stone'.

Michael creates experimental selves and merges with them for the sake of a fuller exploration of what it is to be alive. It's as if he flows into other identities through an osmotic pressure that carries him across the borders that separate and define. In one of his poems, Michael writes: 'I am Proust, de Vigny, Owen Aherne, myself – the identities are interchangeable.' In response to his sense of himself as other, Michael claims the other as self.

Michael is both the singer and the song, creating places in the mind where I'm released from the confines of M Ward and free to imagine other ways of being, other places to be. His poems bring me into a present moment of his life – standing on a platform at Central Station or waking up on a rainy day – and show me a new way of seeing the life that's happening around me.

As I read, I find myself participating in a conversation that's bringing me into a more caring, more passionate and imaginative world than the one I fell out of when Julianne died. Michael's poems become part of my weaponry against the noise in my head. Trying to sleep, I drown out the mind's monologue by reciting my favourite lines.

While Michael identifies with imagined selves in his poetry, and with other fictional or historical figures, I begin to identify with him, to internalise his personae and merge with his psyche. I feel that I know the ebbs and flows of his imagined life as intimately as I know the currents of my own soul. Michael's poetry creates a world for us that's more in line with our romantic dreams than materialistic society. We walk together in this created world, untouchable because we're spoken for and with by poetry. We seem to inhabit the same skin, often exclaiming, in the way that lovers do, how one of us has just said what the other was thinking. It's all or nothing, total immersion. Falling in love is a madness. Not the involuted madness of brokenness and loss, but an inspired, expansive madness. Poetry, music, art, love. You respond to the throb, the pulse, of the god within. Falling in love when you're mad feels sublimely sane.

But the god is capricious. This feeling can disappear in an instant if a cough rakes through Michael's chest, or if the noise breaks through to me, mocking and obscene. We're walking a tightrope. During our moments of greatest inspiration, we're most vulnerable to falling into the wreckage of our mundane selves. Our ecstasy can be ambushed in a flash, the inspiration turned to despair, and this sublime sanity exposed as a malicious lie.

6

Liminal Spaces, October 1972

'The doc says I'll be dead in six months.'

Michael's voice is flat and his eyes search my face for a response. I stare at him.

We're in the corridor outside the men's dormitory. Michael has just returned to M Ward after seeing a doctor in the general hospital about his lung condition and physical health.

I ask him, 'Are you serious?'

'That's what he said. My kidneys are fucked. My lungs are fucked. I'm done for.'

Michael looks down the corridor. I follow his gaze and see the scene as a black-and-white photo in which mannequins stand to attention. A woman leans against the wall. A nurse in white carries a tray. Doors open into shadow.

'What else did the doctor say?' My voice feels like a piece of string in my throat.

Michael mentions his kidneys again and something chronic, an infection, but his eyes are unfocused. Or maybe it's my mind. Everything is blurred. I don't understand; I want an explanation. But Michael just shrugs, holds my gaze for an instant, then looks down. His bony shoulders express a fatalism that makes me weak.

As someone pushes past us, going into the men's dormitory, Michael takes my hand. We walk along the corridor towards the day room.

Michael dead in six months. I can't take this in. I become air. You could put your hand through me.

In the day room, I see the other patients as a cluster of waxwork models posing on the couches and at the tables. As if from above, I see Michael and me looking like a couple of strays. His beanie has slipped forward to his eyebrows, and his shoulders slope at an angle as he leans towards me. I look small beside him, my long hair hanging straight and loose, and my eyes wide open. We're holding hands. It's a film I'm in, but I've forgotten the plot, what's supposed to happen next.

***

The doctor's prognosis seems impossible. I feel I must do something, but I don't know what. My mind has short-circuited; it can't process the idea that Michael could die.

That night and the next day we don't talk about what the doctor said, but we speak of death. Michael tells me that his nights are long and difficult. He talks of having 'the ta-tas' – of wanting to end his life. I don't know what to say. You can't talk reason to death, and sometimes not even love. I just listen to his desperate monologues and speak to him about his poetry and our future together, hoping that he'll find a flicker of hope.

I'm finally coming to realise that he's been in a state of collapse for some time. His self-portraits have been highly romanticised, even those concerning his illness. He's been speaking to me as if his life were imaginary, as if he were a figure in a poem or a story, living down-and-out but revelling in the struggle and transforming it into poetry. Now this gloss has faded, and he lets me see his misery.

The past year has been the worst of his life. It included devastating losses: the death of his father, the ending of his long relationship with the artist Hilary Burns, the sale of the house where they had lived, and a motorbike accident that resulted in severe head injuries and sixty stitches in his leg. While in hospital he was treated with morphine, which re-addicted him to heroin. He then moved to a rented room in inner-city Darlinghurst.

I see the stories of his life as a junkie as if from a distance, as stills from a documentary, too raw and sad to take in close up. Severely depressed, he couldn't read because of the head injury, and he was driven by his addiction. At times he was sick with pleurisy and pneumonia, unable to care for himself. He often spent days alone in his room, but he also hung out with other junkies or spent nights trawling the streets, looking to score drugs, trying to keep out of the way of the police. As he describes these times to me, his despair is palpable. 'Been down so far, don't know if I can pull myself up,' he says.

It's been a day of raw nerves and fractious exchanges on the ward. Michael was drawn into an intense encounter with Sister G, a clash over him forgetting that he had left his clothes in the laundry dryer. And Marie and Brian, two patients in their teens, exploded in an argument. Later, Brian threatened to kill himself, addressing his threats to Michael, who had tried to convince him that things weren't as bad as they seemed.

Now, a new patient paces around the room talking loudly to himself, and Lydia's temper adds to the tension as she rocks on her chair. From time to time she erupts into angry comments directed towards people sitting near her.

We seem to feed off each other's anxieties and tensions in the claustrophobic day room. At times, the atmosphere is overwrought, as if we're all waiting for a reprieve from some imminent catastrophe, waiting for someone to walk in the door with news that a dreaded event hasn't happened after all. Waiting for things to get better.

When everyone has gone to bed, Michael and I sit at a table writing in our notebooks. After a while, he pushes a poem across to me. In the final two verses, he's written:

love
let live
all who are different or strange
cherish your freaks and bastards

o wicked god of love
exquisite joker cruel as traps
release these iron jaws from
memory and from the spirit.

The poem ends with the note: 'Writ in the House of Torment/M Ward, Canberra Hospital.'

'There are only two things that are true,' Michael says. 'Love and suffering.'

I want to comfort him, but I see that writing is the only comfort he craves. We sit in our place next to the stereo and listen to Nina Simone singing Dylan's 'I Shall Be Released'. And I hope for a breakthrough.

***

Two nights after the doctor's prognosis, as we're drinking coffee together in the day room, we talk of Canberra.

'A weird city,' Michael says. 'It's eerie how organised it is. And so clean and neat. But there's something sinister about it.'

'Yeah, like living on a film set,' I say. 'The lifestyle here feels like role-plays.'

'The death style too,' he says, with an offhand laugh.

'Death style?'

'Every city has its own peculiar death style. A Los Angeles death would be by addiction.'

'What about New York?'

'You'd get shot there,' he says.

'Oh, okay. So I guess Sydney would be misadventure, falling from a cliff top–'

'–and the death style of Paris would have to be stylish.'

'It'd probably involve a love triangle.'

'Absolutely, and a duel.' He pauses. 'And Canberra's death style would have to be something hidden and private – suicide by carbon monoxide poisoning.'

I laugh, but our flippancy makes me anxious.

Death feels close to me, as close as life, not something distant and irrelevant. I still carry Julianne's death within me like another self. And, like Michael, I'm a romantic. I understand wanting to sail over the edge of the world or fly into the sun from an excess of life, an intensity of imagining.

This idea of an extinction of self both dazzles and petrifies me. It's part of a formula that equates life with suffering and death with its absence – with freedom, with soaring, with release. But death also means falling, descent, the underworld.

Once the thought of death has lodged in the imagination, it's impossible to ignore. It demands engagement, insists on a response, a dialogue. Michael's poems of death enter into this dialogue, and he tells me that death stalks him. He can't come to terms with the grief he feels for his father. In losing loved ones, we've lost parts of ourselves.

Sometimes there's a jubilant intensity to each breath. At others we're empty and useless as the manic energy of our highs collapses into depressive troughs. We're ecstatic, and we're in despair.

***

A week after his arrival in M Ward, Michael was interviewed by a *Canberra Times* journalist. The article appeared a couple of days later: 'Poet who lives in the underground'. Michael read out bits to me, enjoying what I thought at the time was a rather bleak picture of a brilliant young poet recovering from a heroin addiction.

Now, I read the whole article, a paragraph at a time because of my eyesight. I'm sitting in the day room, across a table from Michael, when I read a detail that he had omitted: that just before his twenty-fourth birthday, only a month or so ago, he swallowed a bottle of sodium amytal 'and waited to die'.

The painting of Ned Kelly in his armour appears in my line of vision as I register the grim intention behind Michael's talk of suicide.

I look over at him, watching as he writes. I see his secretive beauty – the arching eyebrows, the angles of his cheekbones, the curved eyelids. I sense his inwardness.

'What is sodium amytal?' I ask.

He glances up at me. 'The truth drug. It's a barbiturate, a sedative. Heavy stuff.'

'It says here you swallowed a whole bottle.'

'Yeah, had the ta-tas. It was a bad time.'

'You might have died.'

'That was the idea – but here I am,' he says brightly.

I say nothing.

He takes my hand, suddenly serious. 'And here you are,' he says. 'And that changes everything for me.'

'Yes, I am here. I'll always be here. And there's your poetry – no one can take that from you.' There must be something else I can say, some spell I can cast to take away his despair.

'There is that. Wrote some more last night – though you couldn't call them poems. One pointless rave after another.'

'Some poems are raves,' I say. 'Ginsberg's, for example – you could say "Howl" is a rave.'

'Yeah, I guess you could. I'll drink to that.' He takes a swallow of his cold coffee and looks across the room to the stereo. 'Hey, let's put on some music.'

No one replies when he asks the patients sitting nearby if they'd object to him playing Carole King. We listen to *Tapestry,* the sound low. I hold Michael's hand in both of mine and rest my head on his chest. We don't speak.

Love isn't only a feeling, I realise: it's a decision about a way of being, a commitment to living, to each other. After all the talking, we come back to the simplicity of being together now, just us and the music, no past and no future. I'm determined that our love will be stronger than death. Michael's right – the fact that we're together does change everything.

***

A couple of days later, I sit at the breakfast table in the day room waiting for Michael to appear. He's usually here long before now. I ask the Man from Kosciuszko to check the men's dormitory. He's not there. I ask a nurse if she's seen him, but she's only just come on duty. I ask a few patients. Someone says he's sick.

Then Andy, the other recovering addict, tells me that Michael overdosed in the night and was taken to another part of the hospital.

I head straight to the nurses' station. I want information, and I'm not going away until they tell me where he is. When I say I want to see him, they insist I needn't worry, that he's being looked after and isn't allowed visitors. I panic. I repeat that I need to see him. They tell me that it's almost medication time and I should go back to the day room.

I wait at a table with other patients as the medication trolley is brought in. From their chatter, I know it's now all around the ward that Michael overdosed. I'm convinced that he's dead. My mind sifts through the details of yesterday, trying to find some clue, trying to understand what happened.

When the nurses offer me water and tablets, I knock them away. They spill on the floor. I'm shouting, at my wit's end. I want someone to tell me what's going on.

Two nurses escort me to my room, hold me on the bed and pull down my jeans as another nurse injects me with a tranquilliser. I lie on the bed, numb and remote from myself. I'm a pinpoint in a body that feels like stone. Impossible to think of Michael, impossible not to think of him. His absence is a siren I can't turn off.

***

Michael appears and stands in my doorway like an exclamation mark. Two days have passed. 'Been sick,' he says, leaning against the doorframe.

'Sick?' My voice sounds hollow.

I sit up, grab a cushion and hug it to my chest. I stare at him standing there, a ghost of himself, his face drawn and grey, his eyes cloudy. I can't believe what I'm seeing. When he coughs, some part of my mind accepts that he's real, although I can't feel that it's true. My mind is stuck at the crossroads of cognition.

'Feel weak as a kitten,' Michael says. He remains where he is, leaning at an angle to the doorway as if reluctant to enter. He looks as though he'd collapse if I touched him.

'What happened?'

'Nothing really. OD'd. Too many nembies. Not enough nembies.'

I don't reply. The blood drains from my brain. The siren returns.

When he sinks into the chair under the window, I ask him again what happened.

For him, it's simple. He just wanted to be 'out of it' for a while, and was able to score some speed and Nembutal from Andy. Michael's angry that the police were called and that people went through his belongings while he was unconscious. He collapses in his chair like a shadow puppet, all stick legs and arms. When I get up from the bed and place my hand on his shoulder, he leans forward and rests his head in his hands.

***

Although I'm reassured by Michael's presence, his overdose, like the doctor's prognosis, is a shadow hanging over us that we don't discuss. Fear grows in the silences between us. I am so afraid for him, for us.

The day after his return, Michael is again sitting in my easy chair. I've put on a Nina Simone record. He's wearing a faded checked shirt, jeans and boots, and I can see the pointy bones of his knees through the denim. He's just said something and, as he waits for my reply, his eyes rest heavily on me the way they often do, as if they can't bear the weight of what he's thinking. He takes a drag on his cigarette as Simone begins to sing 'Just Like Tom Thumb's Blues'. Her voice is plaintive, the music dirge-like and painful. Michael retreats into a far-off inner place, his eyes becoming small with distance.

It seems that drugs meet a need in him that goes far beyond physical addiction, a need linked to his devotion to Rimbaud's poetry and his idea of what it is to be a poet, his fascination with myths and his identification with mythic figures, Icarus and Leander and other tragic heroes. A need to live beyond himself, escape himself.

But now I find myself looking at him differently, coming to the understanding that he's in the grip of a dangerous and powerful compulsion.

Simone finishes her last song, and we go out for a walk around the lake. The sky is overcast, and at the tip of the peninsula we stand looking into the grey expanse of water. Our conversation skims the surface of our misery, then sinks into silence. Michael hunches his shoulders and closes his eyes as he exhales cigarette smoke. He lets the butt fall to the ground. 'I'm fucked,' he says, grinding it into the dirt with his boot.

I lean into his thin body, and he puts his arm around my shoulders, pulling me close. We hold each other, staring at the lake. Crows are cawing in the gum trees, and useless waves lap against the stone wall at the water's edge. Never in my life have I felt this hopeless.

***

A dull, cold pain has lodged in my chest. I wake up to it in the morning, and it's still there at night when

I'm lying in bed in the darkness. One night, as I'm drifting between sleep and wakefulness, I'm jolted into a memory of lying in my downstairs bedroom at my parents' place. I recognise the pain in my chest – it's been there since Mrs Gilroy rang to tell me Julianne was dead.

All the things I'd known by heart fell away after I heard the news: the smell of the morning, the warmth of family meals, the inwardness of music. In my world, Julianne would soon return. The effort of keeping her alive required all my energy, absorbed every breath. Only the conditioning that preserves social manners and roles kept me going.

I was in shock; the news of Julianne's death failed to penetrate my consciousness. The arc of the event was stilled, like an axe the instant before it falls, its motion stopped in mid-air though its trajectory through space is already drawn. Impossible to go back, impossible to go forward. In this liminal, suspended space, I thought of a stalactite growing for thousands of years in a dark cave. I imagined the slow path of the water hardening along the neck of the icicle-like formation in a slow, repetitive ritual, one drop after the other, dripping endlessly in the darkness. And I grew old in that thought and unbearably tired.

I was moving on the treadmill of ordinary life, fitting my actions to whatever was happening around me. But the axe remained suspended.

I didn't go to Julianne's funeral. I didn't even think to go. I have a vague memory of my mother standing at the kitchen door and asking me if I was going, but I can't remember my response. I only have a sense of myself insisting that everything be just as it had always been. In the reality I'd constructed for myself, there was no funeral to attend. I couldn't experience my grief or share it with others who had loved her, and so that grief turned in on itself, an ouroboros devouring its own tail.

About a week after her death, I was in a lecture theatre waiting for a philosophy class to begin. Julianne and I would normally have been there together. The lecturer entered the room, walked across the podium with his signature silk scarf billowing out behind him, and wrote on the board, *Do I exist?* He then launched into a long summary of Descartes's arguments on existence.

Somewhere around me was a disturbance. Someone was talking loudly, throwing their hands about and shouting at the lecturer. People were turning in their seats, straining to see what was happening. Then I was led outside, and someone drove me home. My mind's wiring had fused and misfired. There was only static and broken sounds coming from a distant transmitter.

When I was a small child, I knew that another world existed beyond the one I was familiar with. The everyday world where people smiled and everything had a place existed only on the surface; day turned into night and morning came again and life resumed its daily routines. But beneath all of this is the world inside darkness. Here you're blind because there's nothing to see, you have no hands because there's nothing to touch, and there's no tongue in your mouth because there are no words and no food. Only your ears let you know you're alive. There are sounds and voices inside the darkness, and silences. And they are all terrifying.

As a child, I'd sensed the world inside darkness while watching bath water whirl down the plughole. I'd felt it as I went to sleep at night.

After that philosophy lecture, I found myself living in that world.

The axe had fallen. The question 'Do I exist?' had cut through my denial, and Julianne's death had become a reality. Madness took over. I paced around the house, wringing my hands and pounding my head to try to stop the noise. I no longer had any idea who I was. I sat in the lounge room, my long hair covering my face, my legs jerking back and forth. The chaos in my head was loud and unremitting.

I don't remember the weeks that followed. Sometime later, I learned that my parents had been advised by a local psychiatrist to take me to a private psychiatric clinic in Sydney rather than M Ward. In the hospital environment, I began to think I was Julianne. I was convinced that, like her, I would be killed by ECT.

And, like her, I couldn't stop talking loudly. Thoughts tore through my mind like a firestorm.

Before Julianne died, I never thought that we could die. Never thought that we could lose ourselves and become mad. After leaving the Sydney clinic, I wrote in my notebook:

> *Death is personal. No one can die for you, or live without you. It's also logical. Death is the ultimate process of elimination.*

I keep going back to Julianne because I can't go back.

***

On the ward, suicide and death are recurring conversation topics. All breakdowns involve a kind of death. Out in the world, people don't talk about it; only the mad and the dying talk about death – and even the dying don't talk about it that much. Here in M Ward, it's risen to the surface from deep in our cultural underworld. With its one living eye, it stares us in the face.

After Michael's overdose, the presence of death is insistent, and for me it signifies far more than simply the end of life, that final breath. Death takes everything away except my life: it's the end of hope and the beginning of the madness that invaded me when Julianne died. Maybe I stole her death from her and made it my own so that I could be closer to her and avoid the burden of myself. The loneliness.

Michael seems to have been in thrall to death for some time, and in him it appears in many guises. Death is an old ruin he's taken shelter in, the end of his search for home. It's a poem he throws away, convinced that poetry has abandoned him. Death is his thin and trembling body, and the cough that saws through it, relentless and mean. When Michael talks of death, he's really talking about his sense that he can't keep on living.

How much of this state is caused by his addiction, and how much is the cause of his addiction? What I know is that death persists in him as a powerful melancholy.

In the face of its presence, we begin to talk of being survivors. We want another chance. In a new poem, Michael writes, 'Survival is the password, spread it around.' And I see that, in a previous one, he had written 'the ultimate commitment is survival'. But while we talk privately about love and the decision to survive, when we're with friends like Kate and Andy, Michael still raves about drugs. I reach for a cigarette and inhale deeply to smother my fear. My faith in our future falters.

I've died to my old life – there's nothing left of the person I was. And I know what it's like to want to die. But since I met Michael, I want to live. I'm occupying a space between a life that's gone and a new life with him. I've invested all my hope in it.

Michael's relationship with death is, I realise, different from mine and far more complicated. He investigates dying in order to discover what it is, what it's meant for. But this implies that there's a choice in his fixation, and I don't think there is.

When I was at school, I had a picture of Saint Michael the Archangel on a small holy card. It represented him as a powerful, winged figure with a sword, threatening the fallen angel Lucifer, who lay defeated at his feet. When I see Michael struggling with the powers of survival and death, I think of this image, and trust that, in the end, it will be the Michael I love holding his sword high in triumph over the cowering angel of death.

In Michael's inner world, the sword he holds is Excalibur. In his poem 'Still Life', dedicated to me, this sword with its Arthurian resonances is turned on himself:

> *i cannot pull the sword out*
> *of the stone to rip*
> *my veins apart.*

I see the effort involved for Michael in defying the death urge. He's in the grip of something beyond my understanding; all his heart's complex yearnings and all his conscious thoughts are united in his attempt to negotiate his way through it.

Sitting in the day room listening to Dylan's album *New Morning,* Michael and I imagine after-death experiences. I remind him of the reference he made to bardo country at our first meeting, and we talk about *The Tibetan Book of the Dead.* We decide that he was right when he saw that M Ward is a place where we wait to be reincarnated. We imagine ourselves as souls travelling together through bardo country, watching visions arise from thoughts we had in this life. We imagine the visions that might be associated with different kinds of thinking – music thoughts, love thoughts, thoughts about dogs. Soon this turns into a game of seeing who can come up with the most absurd vision.

Then Andy joins us, and Michael starts talking about drugs again. He speaks as if being high is like riding a wave to the edge of existence. I remain silent.

In the months when he was using heroin and living in Darlinghurst, Michael got to know other junkies. He tells us of people he knew who died of overdoses. Dreamers and rebels. The heartbroken, the unlucky, the experimenters. Or those who simply didn't care for much beyond the rush of the high. He seems to identify with people on the edge and with their deaths. What strikes me most clearly, though, is the weariness that settles on his face when he comes to the end of this rave. As if he's heard it all before.

That night, Michael writes a poem on the back of a photocopy – it's the image of a miniature statue, the Infant of Prague. He gives it to me.

statue and prayer

of the merciful
infant jesus
we pray together
i cannot stay
is it night
is it day
so stoned it
doesn't matter or what does.

7

The Labyrinth

The week after his overdose, Michael walks out of a meeting with his psychiatrist and tells me he'll be leaving M Ward today.

I'm shocked. I always thought we'd leave together. I suspect he has to go because of his overdose, but he doesn't offer this as an explanation. He's distracted and depressed, and it's obvious that he doesn't want to talk about what's behind this decision.

He says he'll go back to Caloola Farm, about twenty-five miles away near the village of Tharwa. He was staying there before he came to M Ward, and he tells me that the vibe is friendly and the people are cool. The Anglican priest who runs Caloola is an old friend of Michael's who set the place up as a sanctuary for refugees from the city: junkies trying to kick a habit and people who just need to get their heads clear. Michael will help with the farm work and live in one of the huts dotted around the property.

As one, Michael and I walk out the door and take the path to the green bell. We sit with our arms around each other, and I wonder if this is the last time we'll be here together. I feel the gravity of Michael's life, the burden of who he is to himself. He says he can't cope with life, that there's no place for him. I hear a bitterness in his voice, and I wonder how he'll manage outside the ward and how I'll manage without him here.

We've known each other for just over a month, thirty-two days; we've spent thirty of those days together and talked into the nights. The thought of him going grips my heart.

Back in the day room, everything is the same. The fluorescent lights give the space an ashen sheen, the painting of Ned Kelly still hangs on the wall, and patients sit around waiting for something, anything. It's all familiar except Michael's face, which is sculptural and sunken as if I'm already seeing it from a distance. Rough brushstrokes suggest a moustache and beard, and dabs of blue catch the light of his eyes.

'You're preoccupied,' he says, sizing me up.

'I don't like farewells.'

In the hospital foyer, Michael makes some phone calls. It's all arranged. He's leaving straight after lunch, catching the bus to Tharwa.

Sitting at our favourite corner table in the cafeteria, we talk about visits he'll make, letters we'll write, and how we'll soon be living in a place of our own. I am holding myself together, just.

The mood has shifted, as it so often does with Michael. He's now enthusiastic about going back to Caloola to work the land and tend sheep. He talks about becoming strong and fit, and he asks me to call him 'Jack'.

I like the name. It reminds me of my father's generation: down-to-earth, capable, sensitive men who don't take themselves too seriously and have an irreverent sense of humour. With this new name, Michael plans to reinvent himself as a grazier poet, a man of the land. He says he's tired of the old Michael, sick to death of all his worries and problems. I look at him and see a desperation in his desire to walk away from himself. I tell him that I don't want someone completely different – I want to keep some of the old Michael. We decide that I'll call him 'Michael Jack'.

After lunch, he appears in the day room looking like a hippie farmer. He's wearing his favourite outfit of beanie, jeans and air force boots, and his hessian bag is slung over his shoulder. We walk to the foyer, and after kisses and goodbyes, I'm standing outside the hospital under a blue sky, watching him walk along the footpath away from me. He takes a few paces, then turns and walks backwards, waving. As he passes a fence, he does a little jig in his heavy boots, nearly tripping over a low pole.

He calls out as he recovers his balance, 'I'm gonna get strong, get some muscle. You wait and see.'

'I'll write.'

'I'm counting on it.'

He strides off towards the bus stop.

For some moments I can't think what I should be doing. I can't face the people on the ward, so I make my way to the cafeteria. I float along the corridor in a daze, feeling invisible as people bump into me on their way past. In the cafeteria, I buy a coffee but 'our' table is occupied, so I find another one, feeling displaced. When I raise the cup to my lips, my hands are trembling. I think of Michael's hands, shaking as he held his cigarette, shaking when he gripped an album cover. When you hold on too tightly for too long, something gives and the trembling starts.

I imagine sitting next to him on the bus, taking off through the countryside together into our future, but at this moment there's only my shaking cup and the spilled coffee on the saucer. I begin to have difficulty breathing. The emotion I've been holding down since Michael told me he was leaving bursts through. I'm a moth in fright, fluttering my wings but unable to fly. Michael is gone. I must get back to my room.

I tumble along the corridor and plunge into M Ward, past staring eyes and into my room. A mute scream clutches my throat. I open drawers, throw clothes onto the bed, bend to pick up records from the floor. The room is impersonal; it doesn't want me here anymore. It's time. I must leave.

The panic recedes with this conviction, but before I can organise my belongings, two nurses appear, standing like prison guards at the door. The bunch of keys on the belt of the short one looks like a closed fist. 'Paula, what's this? You're not going anywhere,' she says, coming into the room.

This is the first time my freedom to leave the hospital has been questioned. 'I'm leaving,' I say. The effort of asserting my will takes so much energy. I turn back to the bed and begin to fold my clothes.

'You're not scheduled for release, you know that.'

I take a deep breath. 'This is an unlocked ward, and I'm a voluntary patient. I can leave whenever I want.' My body sags like a rag doll. The noise in my head is scornful of my weak voice.

The nurse with the keys gives a meaningful look at her colleague and leaves the room. I turn back to the task at hand. When I find my sarong, I bundle all my clothes into it. Now my possessions are ready to go.

Go where?

A man steps past the nurse into my room. He introduces himself as the doctor on duty and says, 'Okay, you need to think this through.' I face him. Although he isn't a large man, he seems to take up all the space and oxygen in the small room. 'You can be held in the hospital if we consider you're a threat to yourself or others.' He sounds formal and tired, and his eyes roam my face for signs of comprehension, as if he's already explained this a number of times. But this is the first time I've heard it.

'I'm not a threat to myself – or others.' Breath catches in my chest. Each word is an effort.

'Look, you could be considered a threat to yourself. You're scheduled to see Doctor Hawke tomorrow morning. You can discuss plans for leaving the ward then.'

He turns to go, and I stand in the empty room, staring at the bundle of clothes and the records and books. Somewhere deep inside me, beneath the pressure of my chemical straitjacket, I want to scream and not stop screaming. Break windows, kick doors.

***

What am I still doing here in M Ward? When I was brought here, I was totally unable to make decisions. All I knew was that I wanted the madness to stop, but I had no idea how to make that happen. The medical staff seemed to know what to do. I signed forms, had ECT and mostly took the medication. M Ward offered me a place to be when I was in crisis. There was no alternative method of treatment.

Now that the crisis is over, I don't think that the ECT is helping, and I'm not sure about the medication either. My brain feels singed, I'm heavily sedated, and

I'm confused by memory loss. I can't remember the subjects I've been studying or the names of my friends. I forget news my mother brings me about the family and, when she asks, I can't account for the way I spend my time. I still don't have the will and confidence that enables people to appear as themselves and speak of normal things. I'm disconnected from what's known as reality – even from my parents who come regularly to see me, and my brother, Phil, who rides his bike all the way from school to visit.

But Michael has entered my inner world, become part of its system of meaning. He alone understands what's real to me; he acknowledges my reality. He's the bridge between my madness and the world outside. I can speak truly to him.

After talking with him about Julianne and accepting the fact of her death, I've discovered a hard knot of anger at the core of my grief. Although the coroner found that she died from 'poisoning by an overdose of a combination of sedative drugs', no explanation was given. The drugs had been prescribed by her psychiatrists, but no one took responsibility; no one was found negligent. Julianne had said to her mother, 'They're killing me with these drugs, please take me home,' but Mrs Gilroy felt she had to accept the authority of the psychiatrists. Questioning their power seemed, and still seems, impossible. Complaints get no response. No one cares when people die in psychiatric hospitals; there's no concern within society to ensure that thorough enquiries are held into deaths associated with madness, as if these deaths don't matter.

Julianne was diagnosed on the basis of a ten-minute interview. 'Paranoid schizophrenia,' the doctor said. With that judgment, she was claimed by psychiatry. Her passionate spirit was reframed in terms of symptoms that had to be eradicated. Her experiences were recast as signs of illness, and no psychiatrist asked her to tell her story or listened to her opinions about treatment. Her family heard her and loved her; her friends knew who she was. But in the narrow corridors of psychiatry, she was known only by the label she had been assigned. In the end, they took her life from her, they took her from her family, and they haven't been held accountable for what they did.

I want to leave M Ward. I don't want to take any more medication. But I'm afraid of becoming mad again.

Since Michael's departure, I feel as if I'm in a labyrinth, going around in circles, losing my way as I try to avoid the minotaur at its centre. When I panic, the walls become narrow, the paths baffling and intricate, and I imagine that I'll never find my way out, that I'll spend the rest of my days circling around in the darkness.

If I reach the exit, what then? My parents have offered me my old room, but all my instincts tell me that this is a bad idea. My state of mind is likely to disrupt the whole family – but it isn't only that. My parents are stoic, serious. Family is everything to them, and while they insist I'll always have a home under their roof, I know they're anxious about the impact of my lifestyle on my younger siblings. I haven't gone to Mass since my first year at university, and I'm vocal about my views on religion and politics. In their eyes, I've rejected everything they brought me up to believe. It's also clear that they still disapprove of my plan to marry Michael.

They're in an impossible situation: they worry about me, but I can't be the daughter they want; I love them, but I need to find my own place in the world. I'm twenty-three, Michael is twenty-four.

It's time to move on and create a life of my own with him at Jumping Creek. The three months until our wedding seem an eternity.

I still want to avoid conflict with my parents, though. I want to hold on to the bond between us.

***

In the afternoon sunlight I lie on my bed, my mind spinning with memories I haven't thought of for a long time.

Like the time my father and I stayed at Tathra on the south coast of New South Wales. I was nineteen, and I'd recently been released from hospital after my first breakdown. Dad arranged for the two of us to stay at a friend's beach house. This was very unusual: I'd rarely spent time alone with him, as we normally did things together as a family. I felt tentative and awkward as the familiarity of our usual roles gave way to the bare reality of two people sharing a small space for a week.

The holiday house was like the ones we'd stayed in during the summers of my childhood, basic but comfortable. There was lino on the floor and old couches around the walls, a green laminex kitchen table and a radio on the shelf above the bread bin. Our talk was mostly of ordinary things: how the fishing had gone, the weather and the daily routines. Each evening we listened to the news on the radio as Dad prepared the fish we'd caught and I cut up vegetables. After dinner we played card games, mostly rummy and poker. Dad tried to teach me his favourite, five hundred, but I couldn't grasp the rules.

I was heavily medicated on the antipsychotic drugs Largactil and Mellaril. I couldn't read because of their effect on my eyes. My mind was often blank; at other times, it pursued problems that I couldn't possibly solve, like the origin of the universe or the end of human suffering. I became anxious and talkative. Dad negotiated these episodes with a gentle tolerance, not saying much but being attentive. His acceptance of anything I said, however delusional, was like an embrace from a benign beyond. The stranglehold on my mind was loosened, leaving it free for a while from the need to obsess and argue.

For Dad, whatever the season, if you were down the coast you went fishing. During our week at Tathra, we fell into a morning routine of negotiating the rocks until we found a spot where his fisherman's instinct told him we'd catch something. We spent hours attuned to our lines as waves crashed onto the rock shelf and gulls eyed the bait.

On one of those blue-and-white days when sunlight sparkles on the water and wind whips the waves into peaks, Dad was standing close to the edge of the rocks, his line between his fingers. I stood off to his side trying to bait my hook. My hands trembled from the medication and the prospect of putting sharp metal into the flesh of a dead fish. I began to cry as I held the hook in one hand, the bait in the other.

Without comment, Dad gently took the hook from me, baited my line and, with a smooth and arching movement, threw it far out into the water. I stood there next to him on the rocks, feeling the pull and ease of the ocean through the line in my fingers, the wind and the sea spray on my face, and the closeness of Dad beside me. I had the thought that somehow, one day, things would work out.

I think of him now, standing on the rocks along the shoreline, his fingers tending to the line while his mind travels to regions known only to himself.

In my other favourite image of Dad, he's dancing the soft-shoe shuffle in the lounge room singing 'Underneath the Arches', the iconic song of the Great

Depression. It tells of homeless men sleeping beneath a railway bridge, dreaming of the future and remaining optimistic as they make the best of homelessness. The song captures Dad's attitude to life: he relishes being alive. No matter what project he's working on, there are a thousand others he can't wait to get stuck into. And no matter where he travels, there are a hundred other places he'd like to go. Boredom is alien to him.

I remember him sitting down to dinner with us all and saying, with a wry smile, 'I wonder what the poor people are doing tonight.'

But there's a darker side to Dad, one I don't think of that often. Late at night he sometimes sits in his green chair in the corner of the lounge room, a whiskey in his hand, melancholy and inaccessible.

When Dad was quite young, his father was admitted to a psychiatric hospital, the trauma of the war having caught up with him. Dad keeps his feelings about his father's madness and absence from the family to himself. What I know of this time comes from Mum's stories about how Dad shouldered much of the responsibility for the family after his father's breakdown. It was the Depression, and Dad was the second eldest of five children. As a young boy, he grew and sold vegetables to help with the family finances, and he spent cold winter afternoons walking along train tracks, picking up the coal that railway workers threw off the trains for people to collect.

In 1941, when he was nineteen, Dad enlisted in the army and spent over four years at war, mostly fighting Japanese forces in New Guinea. While on a week's leave, he and Mum were married in the church near the kindergarten where they'd first met. By the end of the war, he had a ten-month-old daughter, Irene, whom he'd never met.

Mum has told me the story of how she waited for him on the day he was due home, sitting on the veranda with their baby and his mother. The house was on a corner, so she had a good view down the street to the bus stop. She watched as people got off the bus, walked for a while then disappeared into houses along the way. Buses came and went. She saw someone in uniform but looked beyond him to the others because he seemed like an old man. He had a limp, and he was thin and hunched over, carrying a large kit bag on his shoulders. It was only when he turned to walk in the gate that she recognised him.

Dad has buried his experiences of his childhood and the war in parts of his soul unreachable, perhaps, even to himself. Beyond the roles of the public servant passionate about his work and the responsible family man, he isn't easy to know well. For all his energy and enthusiasm, he's a man who doesn't open up readily about his personal life, although occasionally he lays down the law in the family, brings us into line.

Two years ago, after I'd been living away from home for about a year, I moved into a share house. One night, Dad turned up in a rage. I'd never seen him like that before; I don't think I'd even seen him angry. He'd heard that I was living with three men, so he'd come to take me away. My brother John had come with him, afraid that Dad would have a heart attack – he has a heart condition. Dad insisted that I pack my things and stay at John's place. My housemates were taken aback, and I was mortified, but I obeyed for the sake of Dad's health. As far as he was concerned, I was living in sin with not just one but three men, and he had to save me from humiliation.

I was, in fact, having a relationship with one of my housemates. I'd met him at university. We only ever spoke of Julianne briefly; my unacknowledged grief was a black hole at the centre of our relationship, and after eighteen months we drifted apart.

My parents' world is so different from mine that the idea of telling them about this relationship had never entered my mind. They see my sexuality as sinful; they're ashamed of me. I don't know how I could live with them again. My father, in particular, is here in the labyrinth, fierce and protective, but an obstacle to me finding my way out.

***

Identity is, above all else, a pattern that enables you to have coherent responses to other people and the world around you. Without this pattern, I have to think myself together at every moment. I never know what facial expressions, what actions, what speech will be sane and right. What to do, what to say, how to be? My family, the friends who visit, the nurses – they look at me, waiting for a response. A distant part of my mind issues orders: *smile, say yes, take the medication, nod.*

I'm holding on to my love for Michael as the thread that will help me find my way out of M Ward. But anxiety has made me watchful and cautious. I worry that I could lose him at any time. Day to day, with the arrival of his letters, I monitor the changes in his state of mind.

Michael's overdose jolted me out of the illusion of our union into the realisation that we're separate people. And now that I'm on my own in the ward, I have to take on the burden of my distinct self with all its inadequacies. I'm forced to move from 'we' and 'us' to 'him' and 'me', but I can't remember who I was before I met him.

Memories of him keep me going. The day before he left for Caloola, we were granted leave passes to visit my room at Ursula College to organise my things. I needed to vacate the room, so my parents had offered to take my belongings home once they were packed up. Michael and I joked and fooled around as we swept books off the shelves and emptied the cupboards. The late afternoon light was radiant through the yellow curtains, and the untidy collection of my possessions overflowed from bags on the floor. When we'd finished, Michael and I lay together on the narrow bed. He played with my hair as we talked, twisting it around his fingers and stroking it back from my face.

I want to follow him out of M Ward. But as I weave along the dark paths of the labyrinth, I'm discovering that the minotaur has many faces, many forms. He's the psychiatrist, he's my father, he's ECT and medications, he's my own inability to stand up for myself, he's the absence of a place to move into. Spooked by one shadow after another, I hold on to the thread of my love, trying to solve the problem of how to live.

***

On the day of a scheduled meeting with Doctor Hawke and my parents, Michael rides his motorbike to the hospital from Caloola. I wait at the front doors for him, pacing the foyer. He arrives looking tired, although he hasn't ridden a long way. We don't know what this meeting is about, and it feels as if we're being summoned to account for ourselves.

We walk up to my parents, who are sitting outside the doctor's office. When Michael leans down to greet my mother, she smiles but says nothing – I suspect she's as reluctant to be at this meeting as we are. My father gets to his feet and shakes Michael's hand,

and they stand together, making conversation. Dad is dressed for work in a suit and tie; his short silver hair is oiled down, and his face clean-shaven. Michael, towering over Dad, is wearing his yellow-and-purple beanie, a colourful Nepalese waistcoat and dusty jeans. He carries his bike helmet under his arm, and a small canvas bag is slung over his shoulder. I'm glad to see them talking across their cultural divide.

Once we're all in his office, Doctor Hawke seats himself behind his desk, looking like a judge opening proceedings. Michael, Mum, Dad and I sit down in a row opposite him. I can't see Michael from my chair, and I feel cut off from him and weighed down by the presence of my parents and Doctor Hawke. I can't breathe. I lean forward, unable to sit up straight under the burden of their authority. I feel like a prisoner in the dock, waiting to hear my sentence proclaimed.

Doctor Hawke clears his throat. 'Paula is schizophrenic,' he declares to no one in particular. He goes on to detail my medical condition and treatment as though we aren't already all too aware of it. I begin to feel that his words are a form of treachery committing me to a life in which I'm nothing more than a victim of the chemicals in my brain, a creature with no possibility of self-determination.

'Paula isn't well enough to commit to marriage at this point in time,' my father says. 'We want her to live at home, at least while she's ... unwell.' He sounds concerned and reasonable, but I feel invisible. It seems there's no hope for me. I shouldn't expect to make choices for myself.

The words gathering around me dissolve. I lose the sense of the conversation, and I can't speak. Here in this room with the psychiatrist, my parents and my fiancé, I can't find the language to say what I want to say. I'm doubled over with the effort of trying to drag words from the place in my chest where they're lodged. I can't bear my passivity, my meekness, my failure to speak for myself. It isn't just that words don't come to mind. It's that they don't have the meanings I want them to have.

I'm dispossessed of the power of the word. 'In the beginning was the Word and the Word was with God and the Word was God.' All that power and weight and light are too much for me. If a word is God, how dare I speak? The words I want to say aren't of God; they're of some other power. A dark, chthonic, mad testimony to a new kind of life, to blood and flesh and desire. Sacred profanities. I want to speak words that will unsay the power in this room. I want to say 'night', and let it take me away. Say 'love' without breaking. Say the words traced in rivers. I want to say words that will bring me into the world. I want to break the spell.

I become aware that the focus has switched to Michael. I hear Dad saying, 'I'd like to know how you think you're going to support my daughter.' His voice is severe and insistent, and he turns in his chair to look at Michael.

'I have income from my writing,' Michael says simply. He uncrosses his legs and places both hands flat on his jeans as if to emphasise there's nothing more to be said.

'We aren't saying you can't get married,' Mum tells him, dry and tense. 'We just want you to wait until Paula is well enough.'

I no longer feel that Michael and I are the subject of this conversation. The two people being discussed are clearly incapable of thinking for themselves, making decisions or knowing what they want.

'You will need to consider the practical details involved...' Doctor Hawke outlines the medication regime I must follow once I leave the hospital.

After what feels like an eternity of half-heard conversation, Michael's voice breaks through to me. 'We'll wait three months before we get married,' he says. 'That's what we agreed to, and we'll stick to that.'

I take a deep breath and begin reconnecting to myself.

Not long after Michael's statement, the meeting concludes with Doctor Hawke announcing that I need to stay in hospital for a while yet. In a way, I'm relieved. I don't have the confidence to go out into the world; something is still not right with me.

Michael said he'd come to the meeting if it wasn't going to be heavy. It was heavy. We walk to the foyer with my parents, ignoring the meeting in our forced conversation. The only thing I can think of is that we're now definitely committed to waiting three months until we're married.

In the meantime, I must find the words I need to speak the fragments of my life together. 'Words made flesh', words grounded in my body, my heart, not this Tower of Babel in my mind. Madness doesn't have true language: it has bitterness and fear and confusion. It kills living words, cuts them off at their roots. I am mute in its presence, but somehow I must learn to talk back to the madness. When I can do that, I'll be able to say what I need to say to psychiatrists, to my parents and to a society I don't feel part of. Speak true words. Speak of the secret, forbidden things: grief, loss, anger, madness.

***

While Michael's at Caloola, we write letters to each other almost every day. In the first week, his words reflect a happy and positive frame of mind, and he sends love my way.

> *I love you so intensely that i wish i were still in hospital there to love you and watch over you. My shepherding instincts are for, towards, you.*

You are my love. It (love) grows stronger every hour, every moment. The past and present and future are ours, ours to share and plan for.

The idea of getting married gives us hope and a sense of direction. Michael's now thinking of an official church wedding. He writes, 'How would you feel about St John's here in Canberra? My great-uncle Reg Dransfield was rector there and is buried there ... it's High C of E which is exactly halfway between Catholic and Presbyterian.'

My family will be disappointed that the ceremony isn't Catholic, but there's no way I can stand in front of the altar in a Catholic church and make vows. The Church of England seems a good compromise, and I know Saint John's, a beautiful old stone building with stained-glass windows. I also like Michael's idea that in view of the church wedding, our ceremony at Jumping Creek will become a private, unofficial event: 'We'll have a magic Scarborough Fair ceremony, just you & i & the land & the Lord.'

We're already talking of our lives as a married couple. 'If I had a bad accident,' Michael writes, 'you would get a good widow's pension. Home savings accounts too we'll have.' We're searching for 'somewhere kind', for an escape, somewhere to go when our 'soul is worn out'. A place where life can truly be lived as a poem.

Although Michael has embraced the status of non-conformist, in some moods he no longer wants to be an outsider. I can see his ambivalence about this position. He stands at the gates to the city and feels exiled. He still wishes to be a dissident – but accepted as such. Even more, celebrated. Not cast out.

What would society be without its rebels, its poets and artists? I think of the poem in which Michael wrote, 'love/let live/all who are different or strange'. Those who are misfits, those who question and criticise, those who are simply different – they're the aberrant genotypes of our species.

A park ranger once told me that ten per cent of monarch butterflies take a different migratory path to the main group. He said that if the other ninety per cent were wiped out by an environmental catastrophe, the ten per cent that took the alternative route – the aberrant genotype – would help guarantee the survival of the species. I want to believe that people like Michael and I are aberrant genotypes, and as with the butterflies, our unconventional experiences and paths have some meaning and value. Although it's hard to hold on to this idea in the face of feeling useless and hopeless, in theory I believe that people who are different ensure the vitality of our species.

Michael's sense of not being accepted undermines his confidence in himself and has become a source of pain. But a light shines on the horizon. He seems to think that our marriage will mean a degree of acceptance while allowing love and poetry to remain the focus of his life.

We're clinging to something tied to stability, something enduring, something that represents wholeness, at a time when we're fragile, broken and adrift. In M Ward, though, we faced none of the challenges of the real world. When Michael was here, all we had to do was be together. Our love is a hothouse plant, unfamiliar with harsher climes. We'll need to find, in ourselves, practical skills and inner strength; we'll need to connect enough with external reality to get ourselves a place to live and an income.

Michael writes to me about finding a job, and about his ideas for his new prose book and other writing projects. He has been awarded a Commonwealth Literary Fund grant of $2500 and wants to use the money to pay off his mortgage on Jumping Creek. We'll fix the cottage up and live there on money from his writing and my casual work. I'll take a year off from uni – at the moment I'm not sure if I could manage study, but I'm determined to finish my degree once Michael and I have established our life together.

After less than two weeks at Caloola, though, Michael's letters begin to describe experiences of illness and weariness. He writes of 'freaking out' as he endures the long nights in his small hut, and he describes 'strange, bad days'.

o dearest sweet Paul

I've had a very strange bad day, and night now. Must be my stars out of line. Was violently ill this morning, rested til lunch, washed up all our dishes & spent afternoon and evening with Richard up at the shearing shed ... Haven't a clue what's wrong with me. Perhaps it's pneumonia & kidney disease. Anyway I feel terribly sick...

I'd thought that overall Michael's health was gradually improving, but it seems he's still physically very weak and mentally fragile. He wants to feel the sense of accomplishment that comes with contributing to farm work, but his efforts are taking a toll.

Got the shits real bad, claustrophobia in this tiny hut. Went back down to the homestead & talked farming & psychiatry talk & was given loving help & coffee & a pinch of port to drink. Took a Nardil and all my proper pills. It's like the B.I. shits but have had no speed for a week.

A tone of desperation seeps through Michael's descriptions of his days, and it's becoming obvious that he won't stay long at the farm. We're both standing at the end of a wharf ready to depart, but there's no ship in sight and no place to go.

***

Michael's mother comes to Canberra to see him and have a meeting with his psychiatrist. And she wants to meet me. Michael writes, 'You will meet her, she you, you will love each other. Talked to her for 9 minutes today trunk call. Cost me $2.50 but worth every penny.' This meeting is important to him, and I feel that I need to be sane and composed.

We go out to dinner at the Travelodge Motel. Michael is full of our plans, wanting his mother's approval for the wedding and our move to Jumping Creek. Mrs Dransfield is gracious and interested. She listens carefully to Michael's animated description of the wedding at Saint John's. She is, I think, pleased by the family connection to the church.

Michael is sitting up straight and eagerly outlining the future he's planning with his prospective wife. I'm seeing a new side of him: a coming together of the brilliant young poet, the good son and the conscientious husband-to-be. He's charming and funny as we eat our dinner, and I'm impressed by his vision of our future.

I'm also sitting up straight, putting forward my most rational self. When Mrs Dransfield asks me about my life, I speak of our hopes of living together, along with our plans to travel to Vienna and Greece, possibly India. Michael is her only son, and I'm aware that I'm not exactly the person she would be hoping for as a daughter-in-law. I feel as though I'm tripping up with every sentence I utter.

At one point in the dinner, I see the three of us as if we're actors in a play and I'm watching from the wings. I see in the angle of Mrs Dransfield's head that she isn't taken in by our performances. I think she sees us as romantics, not lacking in dreams but not adequate to the task of making them real.

Afterwards, Michael rides back to the hospital with me in a taxi. He reckons the night has been a great success. I'm not so sure. I used to have a best self that I could produce for such occasions, but now the most I can do is scrape together fragments of a self and hope that it will get me through.

***

My parents agree to Michael and me staying at their house for the weekend. I'm amazed by this shift in their attitude – maybe they're starting to accept us. I apply for a leave pass, and Michael rides in from Caloola. When he arrives, my mother shows him to the front room upstairs, and he throws his shoulder bag and coat over the chair at the desk. I look at the narrow bed that he'll be occupying, and I imagine the impossible: him slipping downstairs and spending the night with me.

After a brief meeting with my brothers on their way out to a party, my parents, Michael and I sit down to eat in the dining room. Dad engages Michael in a discussion about the varieties of fish he's caught off the rocks down the south coast, and Michael talks about the decline of the whaling industry in Bega. The Michael I saw at dinner with his mother reappears; he's on his best behaviour, and his manners are impeccable. He charms Mum – much to her surprise, I think.

During dessert, the conversation turns to poetry. 'So, Michael, what inspires you to write a poem?' Mum asks formally.

'It's hard to say,' he says, wiping his lips with a serviette. 'Anything could inspire me, but it's always something of a surprise.'

'Have you ever written a poem about a gum tree?' she asks.

'No, actually, I haven't.' Michael's tone suggests that he'd definitely consider it.

'Well,' Mum says, putting down her knife and fork and leaning forward, 'if I were a poet, I'd write about gum trees.'

'That would be a fantastic obsession for a poet,' he says, delighted. He's obviously taken by the idea of a poet dedicated to a single topic.

'It *is* a bit of an obsession, I suppose.' Mum smiles. 'When I die, I want to be buried under a gum tree in the bush up the back.'

'What's your favourite type of gum?' Michael asks.

'The ghost gum. There was a pocket of them at Tumbarumba where I spent my holidays as a child. Lovely old trees.'

'I'll write a poem about them for you,' Michael says.

After dinner, Dad and Michael go into the lounge room with their glasses of wine, and Mum and I retreat to the kitchen to do the washing up. During a lull in our conversation, she brings up the subject of me coming home to live. 'I've put your bags from Ursula in your old room downstairs and given it a clean,' she says. 'It's all ready for you.'

'Thanks, Mum,' I say.

Simple as that. It's decided. I'm moving back home after three years of living on my own. It's still not what I want, but there's really no other option. While I'm grateful to have somewhere to go, I feel reined in.

***

As my parents settle into their lounge chairs to watch a TV program, Michael and I come downstairs to my old room. There are no longer any posters on the walls, and my books are still in boxes next to the bookcase, but the eiderdowns on the two single beds are the same. The cave-like feeling from the exposed bricks is familiar. As I sit on one of the beds, Julianne's face appears in my mind's eye. I'm reminded of the two days and nights we spent here as her life fell apart, but I don't want to remember that time. I want to think of the Julianne who lived like an Amazon – bold, curious and courageous inside the music. And I want new memories of this space.

I lock the door behind us, aware of my parents upstairs, then I cover a bedside lamp with a red scarf and light candles and incense. I like the look of the room now in the glowing light, and there's an exhilarating sense of privacy. Michael goes over to a stack of records and flicks through them, choosing some and putting one on the player. He sits at the end of my bed, and we talk, smoke cigarettes and listen to the music.

There are no fluorescent lights, no harsh angles and no dramas. Just the two of us. The mystique of the green bell seeps into this space, making it feel round and familiar. We weave the night around us like a cocoon, fragile and ephemeral, as we sit on my bed together, the sounds of Dylan's *Nashville Skyline* and Simon & Garfunkel's *Sounds of Silence* filling the room. Tonight we can be close and intimate. At last we're truly alone together – at least until Michael has to go upstairs to his room to sleep.

Michael returns to Caloola the next day, and I'm discharged from M Ward after living there for seven weeks. Relieved, in the end, that I have a place to go, I pack up my things and Mum drives me home. All I needed was time with Michael to sense a new beginning. I've emerged into the fresh air, all obstacles dealt with, the necessary compromises made. The future is falling into place – not exactly the way we hoped, but we'll soon be together again, and this time we'll be out in the world. Life is about to open up. The labyrinth is behind me.

8

Back Home, November 1972

Within a week, the stress of being home starts to take its toll. My face aches from the effort of smiling as I try to fit in with my family, with meal rituals and customary ways of relating. Everyone is polite and considerate, and the strain of all this niceness is excruciating. I want to smash something, break through the veneer so that everyone can relax and go back to being themselves. My family tiptoe around me as though I might detonate if they say the wrong thing, or collapse if they bump into me. The spontaneity and looseness I remember has gone. I long to excuse myself and go down to the sanctuary of my room so that they can relax, and I can be alone with the lethargy and depression that has settled in me like a dirge.

The family home is a solid, cream-brick house built in the mid-1960s, with views across to the Brindabella Ranges at the front and the foothills of Mount Majura at the back. At ground level there's a double garage and my room, with wide steps in between leading up to an open porch and the front door. For Mum, buying the house was a dream come true, bringing together her love of the bush with her desire for the suburban quarter-acre block. She knew that this was the house for her when she stood at the kitchen window and looked out onto a spread of gum trees and wattles.

This morning, with Mum out shopping and the boys at school, I sit alone in the dining room eating a late breakfast, kept company by the empty house and its silence. Sunlight streams through the sheer white curtains and shines on the honey-coloured wood of the table in front of me. The carpet swirls in patterns of orange and brown, and the chairs stand upright and formal. It's like a stage set, waiting in readiness for the actors to appear and the drama to begin. I drink my coffee and think of the time when I was at high school and, except for my eldest sister, Irene, we all lived at home, and the house was full of people and activity.

There were eight of us, including Mum and Dad: Irene had entered the Brigidine convent a couple of years before we moved to Hackett. My four brothers played rugby union, Anne and I were on netball teams, and we rode our bikes everywhere. Weekends were a whirl of activity, with friends dropping in, people coming and going, and on weekdays there were routines of meals around the table, homework and washing up. I can almost hear the voices echoing through the house – my brothers yelling out to one another, my mother urging us to hurry up, and my sister Anne singing along with Elvis Presley on her transistor radio as she washes the dishes.

Memories of Saturdays return with a particular immediacy. I hear the noise of the vacuum cleaner and the washing machine, and someone screaming from the shower that the hot water has run out. I think of Jim revving his motorbike in the driveway, Robert rubbing down his horse in the backyard, and Mum in the kitchen, cutting up vegetables for soup and giving instructions to anyone walking through. There was always something happening: doors slamming, the phone ringing, people talking.

And there was always music. As Mum did the housework, she sang along to the war songs of Vera Lynn and to songs from musicals like *Oklahoma, South Pacific* and *The Sound of Music.* In the evenings, Dad would usually sit back in his lounge chair enjoying a glass of wine and some cheese and biscuits as he listened to Louis Armstrong, Nat King Cole and some of the American-Irish songs like 'I'll Take You Home Again, Kathleen' and 'Galway Bay'. I played the pop songs of the 1950s and '60s whenever I got the chance: Gene Pitney, Elvis Presley, Dusty Springfield, the Beatles. I bought *A Hard Day's Night* with money I'd earned from babysitting the neighbours' children and danced to it in my bedroom, singing along until I knew the lyrics off by heart.

As the 1960s progressed, the practice of the nightly family rosary gradually gave way to the pressures of individual schedules and the impact of television. The religious prints on the walls also disappeared over time, superseded by landscapes: paintings of the

Australian bush, mostly featuring Mum's favourite tree. The print of Jesus in Gethsemane that had hung on the wall in the lounge room disappeared without anyone commenting on its absence. The Madonna and Child in the hallway was replaced by photos of the family.

In my early teens, I took a picture down from my bedroom wall that had been a favourite during my childhood. It depicted a guardian angel hovering protectively over a child as she walks across a footbridge suspended above a rocky abyss. I used to gaze at it, imagining myself on the shaky bridge, anxious about the prospect of falling but reassured by the presence of the angel with his enormous wings and gentle eyes.

Eventually, only the matching pictures of the Sacred Hearts remained, hanging above my parents' bed in the room at the end of the hall. In one, Jesus points to his bleeding heart; in the other, Our Lady holds her shawl aside to expose her heart as she gazes sorrowfully into the distance.

Growing up, I was always being told what a big, happy family I came from, and this became important to my sense of identity. I congratulated myself on coming from a happy home, and except for the occasional beltings when we were younger and arguments during our teens, it was. But the usual unhappiness and conflict that's part of life wasn't admitted, not openly. We all hid our heartaches and disappointments. Whatever was happening, we smiled through it.

Anger wasn't tolerated, though on rare occasions it burst through. Our parents never argued or raised their voices to each other, and we didn't raise our voices to them. Occasionally a door was slammed, and if Mum was upset with someone, an oppressive silence descended on the house. There were also times when I stormed off into the bush as a teenager or hid myself in my room with a book, but the direct expression of negative emotion wasn't acceptable. Our response to conflict was to withdraw, repress, adapt.

Endurance was particularly admired. Hardship and suffering were to be borne in private, without comment. No matter the crisis, it was important that we 'got on with things'. We were like colourful boats bobbing around in the sunshine on a sea of submerged emotion.

My mother was just as resilient as my father. She once told me a story from her childhood. She was five years old, distressed because she had fallen over and her knee was bleeding. Pop, unemployed and disabled, said to her, 'Come on now, soldiers don't cry.' When she told me this, I thought of him in the trenches hearing the sounds of his mates dying in the fields nearby and suffering the pain of his wounded leg. Not crying. Not feeling. And I thought of her as a little child, learning the lesson.

Experiences of war have also impacted deeply on my father's life, though he's rarely spoken of them. During the war, he was responsible for telegraphic communications back to headquarters and had to go ahead of the company into enemy territory to lay down the telegraph wires. Once the company had taken that section of land, messages could be sent back down the line. It was extremely dangerous work. In one brief anecdote, he told us that his battalion had been transported to Sananada in New Guinea in seven war planes, but only one was needed to bring back the survivors.

Mum and Dad are constitutionally cheerful, and their capacity for optimism created a dynamic home life for us when we were growing up. I know that I was often animated by their energy. But when I was a child, I also found myself inexplicably anxious and sad, and I was ashamed of the way that my darker feelings made me an outsider, someone apart and alone within the family. Those feelings were drowned in the currents that flowed beneath our lives.

The year after my first breakdown, when I was nineteen, I returned home from the hospital and faced the realities of a fragmented mind. Still in shock from Julianne's death and unreachable, I no longer felt 'at home'. My withdrawn mood and my agitation unsettled the family then, just as they're doing now. It's as though I've become the face of darkness in the house. I've always been an introvert among extroverts, but now I need a different environment in which to face my struggle to discover myself and find some sanity. I have to work out how to deal with the dissonance between the weight of my psyche, and the normality and lightness in the house.

For three years before my admission to M Ward, I came and went as I liked, and I created living spaces that allowed me to shut myself away when I needed to be alone. In 1971, I had a room at Lennox House, an old workers' hostel that had been converted into cheap accommodation for students in the 1960s; I also lived in share houses and at Ursula College. Now things are different, and I see that the family home represents an identity I need to leave behind me, a smiling persona that's like an albatross around my neck.

Over coffee I sit in the airy dining room, turned in on myself. My inner world is dark and chaotic, as is my room downstairs. Sometimes I wonder if I'll ever emerge into the light, into a world that isn't dense with imaginings and intense emotion.

***

One afternoon a letter arrives from Michael. I open it eagerly, recognising his spidery handwriting on the envelope. Inside he has written the date: 'midnight, eve of Armistice Day, 10 November 1972'.

> *It's late. my pills aren't working so I've taken more. Not enough, just enough, maybe. Got the shits, the ta-ta's. Lonesome is my mountain hut,*

everything working for me & nothing working for me. I work hard every day & it's a long day & it's a long night to come home every dusk ... I wish I could live to be with you now...

Tomorrow (today now) is Armistice Day. I was feeding a lamb tonight with its bottle and for no apparent reason I started to cry. Dad died on the 26th of this month last year. You are the only thing I bother living for. Literature & grants and sales make me momentarily excited, often for several hours. But it's the same me, scrambled brains & uselessly useful body. It's so hard staying alive. If it weren't for you I'd give living a miss. It's all too much. I get badly suicidal every night! Richard & Carla are good to me but life without you is really 'scraping existence from day to day.' ... What a joke. All i have is you, is yours...

Please be with me all day on the 26th of this month, i'll have a sad bad day, & night especially. Perhaps i could stay at your place (apart i guess) that night & you talk to me and get me through...

I call Caloola right away, but the phone rings out and my panic increases. Phrases from Michael's letter repeat in my mind. He puts all his energy into trying to make a life, but he's an instrument tuned to a minor key, and his tenderness, his melancholy, is heart-breaking. I take off through the backyard into the bush. I have to move. I rush along the track that leads through gums and acacias to the top of Mount Majura.

I don't know what to do in response to his sorrow, his hopelessness. His faith in me only makes me fearful. How can I become strong enough to give him the support he needs? In M Ward, I was there with him when he felt desperate; from a distance, I just don't know how to help him. His grief drags him into a deep place within himself where all his sufferings converge: a crucible of loss and doubt and anguish.

He's obviously in a critical state. As I stumble up the steep track to the mountaintop, I want to shout, send out a distress signal, a flare: *Help! Help! We have an emergency!* But that's not how it works in this sort of ongoing crisis.

I'm useless. I don't feel I'm substantial enough to keep him alive. I don't even have the energy to get to the top of Mount Majura. I find a grassy slope and sit there, exhausted, my mouth dry, breathing hard.

When I return to my room, I read and reread his letter, trying to think of what to do. I look at the poster I've put up on my wall entitled *Desiderata.* 'You are a child of the universe,' it proclaims. 'You have a right to be here.' It doesn't feel like that for either of us, but particularly Michael. I go upstairs and call him again. He's not available, so I leave a message: 'Please come to Hackett tomorrow.'

***

Next day, Michael rings from Tharwa to let me know he's on his way. When he rides up on his motorbike, I'm sitting on the front steps waiting for him. He parks next to the porch, takes off his helmet and shakes his hair free. When we hug I let go of my anxiety for a moment, pressing my face into the curve of his chest, into the musky smell of cigarette smoke and dust. He feels real and present, and I feel weak with relief.

'How's things?' I ask.

'Yeah, good, but I'm thirsty. Any chance of a cuppa?'

We go upstairs, tentatively negotiating around each other as we try to knit together the loose ends of our time apart. Michael is hard to reach, and I'm tight with anxiety again.

'I got your letter,' I say. 'Sounds like things are pretty bad.'

'It was a long night. Can't take these sorts of nights anymore, Pauls, just can't take them. But it's okay now, we're here. It's cool.'

'We'll be together for the twenty-sixth, for your father. Stay here. We'll get through it together.'

'Yeah, thanks, that'd be good.' Michael looks away through the window to the bush outside and sips his tea.

'Written any poems?' I ask after a while.

'Nah, nothing you'd call poetry.'

A silence settles on us. Over our cups of tea we try to make conversation, shrink the distance dividing us, but our reunion is strained. Michael says he needs to leave Caloola but hasn't found a place to live in Canberra yet. In the quiet between stilted exchanges, we hear the clinking of dishes from the adjoining kitchen as Mum does the washing up.

In the afternoon we wander through the bush around the foothills of Mount Majura. Michael spots a tree next to a dam and spreads his jacket in its shade. As we sit there, I remember the times we sat inside the green bell talking, making plans, holding each other. Now, our talk is soft and desultory. Words seem inadequate. More silences shape the conversation. Michael is subdued, and I'm faltering. Just being with him is enough to open me to joy again, but it's a small, hopeless sort of joy.

I study the shadows of the tree on his face, breathe in his smell, enjoy his voice. I'm somewhat reassured by his presence, but during the pauses in our conversation, phrases from his letter repeat in my mind. *It's so hard staying alive.* The pale light of the sky plays on the surface of the muddy dam, and birds call out in the stillness. I lay my head on Michael's chest, listening to the rhythm of his heartbeat, feeling his despair. My love is also my pain, and I don't know how to reconcile myself to the contradiction.

***

After dinner that night, we go down to my room. My parents seem happy for us to spend a few hours here together before Michael goes back upstairs. He takes my old photo albums down from my shelves and insists on looking through them. Family scenes in black and white describe the passage of my childhood. Michael and I sit on my bed, the albums open across our laps, watching a skinny little kid in shorts turn into an awkward adolescent in a beanie and scarf. Michael teases me. 'You were such a smiley, pie-faced kid,' he says. 'Looks like you ran wild.'

He particularly likes the photos of my family taken at Patonga near the Hawkesbury River, where we had a beach shack built by my grandfather and a friend. Michael's curious, so I tell him stories of times we spent there, becoming more and more caught up in the memories as I describe the place and our escapades. The shack consisted of a large room surrounded on three sides by a wide veranda open to the elements from waist height, and it overflowed with children – our family, another family of five children, and two brothers, Frankie and Malcolm, from the boys' home at Westmead.

We slept on camp stretchers on the open veranda, and in the morning we folded them up to make space for playing. At night I'd look out at the stars, listening to the cries of gulls, the pounding surf from the other side of the peninsula, and the wind whipping through the bushes along Patonga Creek. I felt an awe that lifted me beyond myself and overwhelmed me. I felt small and huge at the same time, my heart beating beneath my pyjama top.

In the day, I was one of a loose band of wayward kids. Once we learned to swim, at about age four or five, we could go off for the day with the older kids. For the swimming test, Dad would hold us over the side of the rowboat with a rope around our chests while we swam along, kicking our feet hard.

As I describe these childhood holidays to Michael, the grey cloud that had weighed on us during the day dissipates, and our mood lifts. I'm feeling traces of the excitement and happiness I felt at Patonga, and Michael wants me to tell him more stories of our time there. It surprises me how vivid the memories are and how immediate the feelings. I tell him of swimming in the tidal creek until we were sunburned and sleepy and our skin tasted of sand and salt. The exhilaration of chasing schools of blue soldier crabs, watching them disappear into the holes they dug in the sand with their stick-like legs. The dreaminess of wandering along the beach, collecting shells and driftwood to take home. And the fun of fishing from the wharf with Dad, catching flathead off the sandbanks at the Point and rowing up to the mangroves in a neighbour's boat. I would drag my hand in the water, watching the reeds waving in the slanting rays of sunlight below.

I describe to Michael the trees I climbed to find a solitary place to read and daydream. And I tell him about searching for little frogs under rocks near a creek, and the reaction when I tipped a bucket of them onto the floor of the town post office. I don't know why I did that, but I remember the commotion and my excitement as dozens of frogs jumped around the floor, people yelling and squealing.

I ask Michael if he, too, ran wild as a kid. 'In my mind I did,' he says. 'I was already writing poems and sending them into *The Argonauts* when I was seven. The most exciting thing for me was getting my poem read on the radio one afternoon.'

I try to draw Michael out about these poems, but he just wants me to tell him more about Patonga. It's then that I remember our family's five minutes of fame.

Dad had taken us for a walk around the cliffs one afternoon. We played in the rock pools, looking for crabs and sea snails in the crevices, laughing when we busted the beads on seaweed necklaces and water squirted out. But then Dad started herding us close to the bottom of the cliff, trying to get us to hurry as the sea rushed in over the rocks. I could tell he was alarmed. The sea had cut off our way around to the beach, and Dad insisted we climb the cliff-face before the whole rock shelf was submerged.

I scrambled up through the small scratchy bushes, with Dad helping me find places for my bare feet to push off from. Somehow, one by one, Dad got us all to the top. By then it was late afternoon, and the bush was dense, the area rocky. We tramped through the scrub, keeping close to Dad, collecting wood for a fire. Later, we lined up facing the sea, cooeeing in our loudest voices as we waved our shirts above our heads. I remember the exhilaration of the adventure and my fear, especially when it got dark.

Dad made a huge fire using his matches and a detective novel he'd brought in his back pocket with his tobacco. The fire was seen by people on a fishing boat, and the alarm went out. It was after midnight when we got home. Mum made a pot of tea and a huge pile of toast dripping with jam and butter. We were ravenous. The next day, our adventure was reported on page three of a Sydney newspaper under the headline 'Family Stranded on Lion Island'. I couldn't understand how the paper had got it so wrong, and I wanted Dad to tell them we'd just been caught out by the tide on the mainland.

Inspired by the memory of tea and toast, I put together a snack for Michael and me. We make plans to go to Patonga and explore the Hawkesbury River, writing poems of our journey. We've emerged from our despair. When Michael goes upstairs to the spare room, I go to bed and fall asleep, grateful for this temporary reprieve.

***

With every parting from Michael, there's a wrench, an anguish. When he leaves the following morning, I return to my room feeling emptied out. The image of him riding away down the road on his Kawasaki, the oversized helmet perched on top of his thin, upright back, stays with me. There's something in it of that Nolan print of Ned Kelly: his back to me, the helmet, and him disappearing towards the horizon.

My room with its small window and exposed brick walls is dark and empty without him here. I think of him in his hut at Caloola, feeling restless and claustrophobic as he struggles through the nights, and I can't sit still. I tidy my room. Return clothes to drawers and cupboards. Stand books and records upright on the shelves. Move my record player to a side table. I'm able to deal with the chaos in my room, but I have no notion of how to deal with Michael's state of mind, or my own.

I don't like the word 'depression' – it makes me think of a dip in a bitumen road. I prefer to think I'm sad. My heart is heavy. I'm despondent, dispirited, disconsolate. I'm dreary, dull, miserable. I've got the blues. But these words are somehow too resonant and graphic for the thick, slow state I'm in now. I accept that it's more true to say that I'm depressed. I can't bring any light into my life, and I can't get up in the morning. I'm a dip in a bitumen road.

I can't stop thinking of Michael's last letter to me, of his struggle to stay alive. He has put all his faith in me, and I don't know if he realises I'm just not that strong.

***

I sit at the table in my aunt's dining room in Carlingford, Sydney, surrounded by my grandmother, aunt and uncle, and my mother. I stare absently out the window at the row of pink azaleas in the garden. They're so perfect, they don't look real, but nothing does these days. I'm living in a film of my life. After a couple of weeks at home, I agreed to come with Mum to visit family in Sydney, thinking it might inject some life into me, but I'm lost, unable to contribute to the conversation.

My grandmother looks like the picture of a grandmother, like the Queen Mother. She's wearing a blue dress and a pearl necklace, and her silver hair is curled and neat. When we arrived I wanted to bend down and hug her, but she's so small I thought I might break her. Now I notice her bright, bird-like eyes as she sips her tea. They miss nothing. Not my discomfort or the uselessness of my hands, moving from the table to my lap and then under my arms as she tells us about a recent tennis match that she watched on television. The discussion turns to Evonne Goolagong's chances of winning the Australian Open. I become aware that my tea is cold and my piece of sponge cake is untouched. It's just too perfect to bite into.

No one is looking at me, and I can't look at them. In spite of the lively discussion, there's an awkward energy around the table. The faces of people I've known and loved all my life seem strange. My mind retreats into a baffled, distant region of itself. I drift in and out of the conversation, attempting to follow what's being said but losing track, slipping off into random images. The geometrical pattern of the lino. The photo of my grandfather on the dresser. The handle on a drawer. Or I slip into the dark fantasies of my inner world and stare into the distance. I can't focus on anything for long. Something catches my eye, or a thought trips up my mind, and I forget where I am.

A phone call from Michael brings me back to myself. As my aunt hands me the receiver, I realise that she hasn't been told that I'm engaged, and I haven't told her myself.

'Where are you?' I ask Michael. I need to be able to see him to make his voice real.

'Tharwa. The booth outside the post office. Had to beg for change. How's Sydney?' His voice crackles through the line.

'It's awful. I'm missing you. What's happening?'

'You wouldn't want to know. I'm a total wreck. Hit rock bottom last night. There's–'

'I can hardly hear you, the line's breaking up. What did you say?'

'Nothing. Nothing. You're too far away anyway. I've got the horrors, Pauls. Haven't slept the last two nights. Got a bit of sleep last night, but woke up in a sweat about three. I had this dream, dead birds falling from the sky. Horrible feeling, hollow, there isn't any–'

'I didn't catch that. Can you hear me?'

'Just putting in more coins, hang on ... All done.'

'You sound awful, babe. What a horrible dream. Have you talked to Richard?'

'Everything I say makes me feel like a fool ... claustrophobic ... Don't think I can–'

'The line's cutting out, I can't hear you properly. Sounds like you're on the edge. Come stay at my place.'

'Yeah, I'll come in. When will you be back?'

'Monday. Just remember–'

'What was that? Can't hear you. Forget it. What're you up to?' His voice is as thin as wire.

'I love you. Think of you all the time. Wish I was with you.'

'Come back. I have a–'

Dial tone.

My cousin's room is fairy-floss pink and white, and I'm sitting on the bed, doubled up with helplessness and longing. Phrases from my conversation with

Michael sound ominous as they return to me, disconnected and broken. I think of him standing in the phone booth, the dead birds of his dream falling from the sky, and I want to know what he was going to say when the line cut out.

The slow work of getting through the rest of the day takes all my energy as I try to resist the sedative effects of the medication and the fall into circular, self-pitying introspection. After dinner I try to phone Michael at the farm, but the line is engaged.

That night I keep waking up from a nightmare involving an organ grinder playing music faster and faster until it sounds like a siren. In the morning I send Michael a telegram, conveying my love, as specified, in 'ten words or less'.

***

Home from Sydney, I play the music I love, but it either overwhelms me with misery or I can't relate to it. The emotional rawness of Nina Simone's voice is too painful, and Vivaldi's music creates a world I can't enter. Only Dylan reaches through to me, though there's no comfort in listening to his songs, just familiarity and nostalgia.

I'm no longer deluded, and I'm not suffering from hallucinations, but the depression I'm in will not shift. I'm also having problems adjusting to my new medication. I was suffering negative side effects from the previous drugs, so I'm now taking Stelazine and

Cogentin as well as Largactil. They slow everything down so that emotions and reactions are sluggish and thick, but they also put me on edge, make my nerves jangly and irritable. My nervous system seems to tingle unpleasantly with mild electric charges – but in the ocean of my mind, thoughts drift like debris.

No amount of counting my blessings makes any difference to my defeated lethargy. For hours I lie on my bed like a corpse in the darkness. Eventually I'm able to direct my limbs to move. Brush my hair. Go upstairs. Eat dinner with the family. Stare at the television. A mannequin at home.

One afternoon I manage to catch a bus into Civic and walk over to the ANU library to borrow some books. The supplementary exams I need to sit if I want to pass my year at university are coming up next month, and I've decided that I want to take them after all; I don't want to add yet another year to my degree. But at the library I can't read well enough to find book titles in the catalogue, let alone study. The medication is still affecting my eyesight. Words still blur on the page. I can only focus for a few minutes, and I can't take anything in. My plans are nonsense.

Life in the world demands action, competence, decision-making – all abilities I strive unsuccessfully to find in myself. The wild energy swings of M Ward have passed, and everything seems flat and closed off. Where once Michael and I shared every nuance in our feelings and thoughts, now we have to organise meeting places and navigate issues of transport before we can even begin to talk. Such logistical problems confuse me. In the face of these complications, my sedated mind wants to shut down, turn to the wall, sleep.

9

Village Life

Towards the end of November, Michael finds a new place to live. He's given the key to a room at Lennox House, where I lived for a year before moving to Ursula College, and we can't believe our luck. With this move to Canberra, there's some progress in our lives at last. Lennox is just up the peninsula from the hospital, and although it's two bus rides from my parents' house, we're excited to be closer to each other.

Lennox consists of a series of low, rather dilapidated wooden buildings that settle comfortably into the remains of an old garden dotted with trees, shrubs and patches of lawn. Life there is loose and communal. Some rooms are empty during the summer break, and Michael's going to live there until the beginning of the next university year.

He has been welcomed by Chris Ash and Simon Clough, friends of mine from the time I lived at Lennox. They met Michael when they visited me in M Ward, and it seems serendipitous that he's now living down the hall from them, just metres from my old room. Chris is a Buddhist and Simon is studying law, and Michael's already their friend.

One warm and sunny afternoon, Michael and I are sitting on the veranda at Lennox with Simon, Chris and a group of other residents. Songs from a Crosby, Stills, Nash & Young album are drifting from someone's room. Michael's arm is around my shoulders, and I lean into him, my body curving to fit the arc of his chest, feeling at home with him again. There's an easy camaraderie in the group, and it rubs off on me. People are coming and going, randomly joining in conversations. Slow and casual talk flows along the shady veranda, while out on the lawn a political discussion is becoming animated. Gough Whitlam has just won the election, and everyone is excited about the changes that the Labor Party has promised to make. There's a buzz in the air. Whitlam has announced that Australian troops will be withdrawn from Vietnam: the war is ending at long last.

I've been cut off from politics for months now, and this expansive mood is lifting the fog in my brain. There's a sense that we all have the same political views and are part of the changes that are just around the bend.

The ritual of sharing a joint seems to bring people together, create a group consensus. Marijuana has come to signify not only a person's political position but also tastes in music and dress, and stances on a range of moral issues. People tend to assume that because they get high together, they all share a worldview – and somehow, by association, I'm included. I sink into the collective hum, quiet and peaceful, enjoying the relaxed atmosphere of the afternoon.

The conversation moves to a discussion of the virtues of various drugs. I listen to enthusiastic testimonials, but I still don't think that drugs are for me. I fear that they would unlock a Pandora's box and mad sprites would fill my head.

But I can't help being curious. I want to at least try marijuana again in order to really understand Michael's zeal for it. I'm also interested in the idea that LSD can 'cleanse the doors of perception', and I wonder if it would help me to see the world as infinite and eternal, like William Blake did. I want to be liberated from my narrow and restricted viewpoint – just not right now. So I pass the joint on and instead take a drag on my cigarette.

As people begin to feel the heat in the afternoon sun, they gravitate to the area where the shade of the veranda meets the shade of a plum tree. Talk moves from complaints about the quality of dope being sold in the university bar to an argument about the relative genius of Bob Dylan and Jimi Hendrix. I listen but don't say much. The sun is shining, music is playing, Michael is here with me. I breathe in, breathe out. I see the green light playing on the leaves of the plum tree, I hear a lightness in the voices rising and falling, and I sense my life out in the world with Michael is just beginning.

People wander off during the evening, disappearing into their rooms or along University Avenue to the Union Bar. Feeling hungry, Michael and I stroll through the trees down to the hospital cafeteria, high on the mood of the afternoon. The cafeteria is the only place close to Lennox where we can get something to eat, so it's practically our local restaurant now. We bump into Sally coming in for her shift. She makes a joke about the nights when we slipped away from M Ward, and she invites us to visit her and our friends there. We decide not to – our easy state of mind wouldn't survive the bleak atmosphere of the day room.

It's dark by the time we get back to Lennox. As we walk towards Michael's room, I see a motorbike parked next to the railing and a man sitting on the steps under a veranda light. When Michael asks me to wait in his room, I suspect he's buying drugs and doesn't want me to be involved. Afterwards, as I put on the electric kettle for coffee and chat about the afternoon, I sense a change in Michael's mood. He's restless. We move around each other awkwardly until it becomes clear to me that he wants to be alone. I decide to leave, and we walk under the street lamps to the bus stop. We're holding hands, but our conversation has large holes in it, and although Michael stays with me until the bus comes, I can tell he's anxious to get back to his room.

On the bus heading home, I think about the parts of his life that Michael doesn't want to share with me. I'll need to adjust to a different sort of relationship now we're out of the protected environment of M Ward. The fact is, I don't really understand the role that drugs play in his life. He talks of wanting to stay clear of them, but at the same time he craves them and seeks them out. The 'yes' fighting the 'no', the desire in conflict with the intention. The crucible of addiction. For Michael the need may be more psychological than physical, but at this point in his life, drugs are an obsession. I try to convince myself that the meeting with the biker was just a dope deal, but I'm worried that Michael wants something stronger.

I think of his desire to be Jack, his attempt to get away from the 'drug poet' identity, to get clean and healthy, break free of feelings that keep him trapped in his idea of himself as worn out, wasted, useless – the image he has of himself when he's suicidal. 'Jack' is associated with times he feels optimistic, confident of his poetry, and strong.

At the end of loving notes that he leaves me, he signs himself 'Jack'. Once, after an all-night session with friends at Lennox House, he rode his bike to Hackett and slipped a note under my door. He'd drawn a cartoon of us on his Kawasaki, and another of him wearing a hat, his long curly hair covering his body, his arms outstretched. There's a speech bubble with 'wed me' written inside it. He has signed the note *Michael Jack,* with *Jack* written large and underlined.

I decide that I'll try to call him 'Jack' rather than 'Michael Jack'. It might help him make the transition to a new identity.

***

After only a few days, both Michael and his possessions seem to belong at Lennox – and he's found a spot at the end of the veranda to park his Kawasaki. He's made friends with the other residents, and is spending a lot of time with Simon and Chris, who enjoy his humour and enthusiastic raves. They're also supportive of him, recognising that he's psychologically strung out. One night recently he was particularly depressed, convinced that he couldn't go on living, that he didn't have it in him to face another day. Chris talked him through it, offering the comfort of friendship and conversation.

A few times, after an afternoon at Lennox, Simon cooks up healthy vegetarian meals for us, and we talk about politics, sure that humanity is on the verge of a breakthrough to a new level of consciousness. Simon has a large collection of blues records, so we listen to Billie Holiday and Bessie Smith as we sit together in his small room, sharing stories, laughing at ourselves, believing in love and the future. Both Chris and Simon have a subtle way about them and many interests in common with Michael, particularly music and ideas about the green revolution, and when Michael's mood is free and easy, the conversation is animated, laced with humour and enthusiasm.

Then, late one afternoon, Michael rings me and tells me that he's had some bad news. His friend, Charles Buckmaster, a young Melbourne poet, has taken his life.

I catch the bus to Lennox, fearful for Michael. We sit in his room, and he talks about Charles's last visit to Sydney. He tells me rambling stories of all-night conversations about poetry and life that are now agonising for him to remember. Charles's death confounds Michael, challenging his sense that it's his responsibility as a poet to live without a safety net, to push boundaries, to seek out new modes of poetic consciousness through whatever means he can, whatever the cost.

A kind of vicarious grief eats away at me as I helplessly give him my sympathy. We lie on his bed holding each other as the room gets dark. 'Too many deaths, too much loss,' he says. 'They take so much of me with them, there's nothing left.'

I feel I have no words to offer him, no comfort I can give.

After a last cup of coffee, I decide to leave, and Michael offers me a lift home on his Kawasaki. The thought of riding into the night brings a sense of release from the grief of the day. We take off along University Avenue under the dark forms of oaks and silver poplars, round past the Academy of Science, taking the curves like dancers leaning into the wind.

One sharp bend feels too fast, too wild. I clutch Michael tight, but wind whips my face, my hair, and there's no ground beneath me. I'm not breathing. As we take another bend, tilting into the road, I'm sure I'm going to die. We weave around cars – he's going the long way to avoid the lights – and I'm frozen with terror. When he pulls up in the driveway at home, I can barely step off the bike. Feeling sick, I sit on the steps, shaking and mute.

Michael says that he wasn't going too fast, and it's true. Something just freaked me out. I'm unnerved by Charles's death; it feels ominous. But I can't explain what happened, and I feel weak and miserable that I've added my neurotic fears to the desperate emotion of Michael's day.

Before he leaves, he holds me for a long time, his hand pressing the back of my head against his chest, his body close. We don't say much. He revs his bike and takes off down the road. I go into my room, close the door. I have a desperate need to sleep. As I lie in bed, I try to draw on memories of us in the green bell, but all I feel is a sense of something collapsing inwards, smothering us.

***

Michael's room at Lennox smells of stale incense and cigarette smoke. It's late afternoon. He's lying on the bed, and I'm sitting near him, smoking a cigarette. A blind is at an angle across the window, and the room feels empty, abandoned. Michael's coat hangs on a hook on the back of the door, and his air force boots lie discarded next to the desk.

My cigarette smoke swirls through shards of late afternoon light as if through river water. I find myself thinking about drowning, how it might feel. The pressure on the chest, the panic, then the letting go into release and oblivion. Outside, parrots are screeching in the plum tree, competing with the sound of someone playing guitar in the adjoining room. The guitarist is learning Dylan's 'Boots of Spanish Leather'. They sing a line, stop, repeat it, correcting a chord, then the tedious repetitions and interruptions begin again.

I've been here for a couple of hours, dipping into a Raymond Chandler novel that I found on the desk. I'm restless and anxious; I don't know whether to leave or stay. Michael is fully dressed, still wearing his beanie, his face turned towards me. He's not asleep, but neither is he awake. He looks peaceful, and I don't want to intrude, but I don't know how long he's been like this or what he's taken, and I'm worried. I lie down beside him and ask him again if he's okay. He finds my hand and squeezes it weakly.

Later, I rinse a cup in the corner sink and make myself a coffee. As I smoke another cigarette, I realise that the guitarist has stopped playing and the parrots have fallen silent.

When darkness seeps into the room, I get up and turn on the desk lamp, creating an oval of yellow light that gives the impression I'm on a small boat, drifting at sea. A few scattered books and papers, a coffee mug, a red Swiss Army knife clutter the deck, and Michael's blue paisley headband hangs motionless from the back of a chair. I'm becalmed. In the doldrums. I pick up another book from the desk and flip through the pages before putting it down again. When I touch Michael lightly on the shoulder, he shifts onto his back, and I think I see the trace of a smile on his face.

I lie down next to him again, listening with my body to his breathing. I surrender to the sequence, in and out, until I'm breathing for us both, pacing my deeper breath to his shallow rhythm. For the moment after each out-breath, time stands still. We are held in the deflated space of no-breath, no movement, no life. Then we breathe in, and the waiting seeps through me again, like mercury flowing in my veins.

***

After Christmas, Michael moves out of Lennox House and goes to live with Simon in Hall, a village outside Canberra. Simon's bungalow is on the edge of town, overlooking grassy hills that disappear into the Brindabella Ranges. Michael keeps his room at Lennox so he'll have somewhere to crash after parties, but Simon's place is now home.

Richard Hopkinson, an old friend of Michael's, has arrived from Sydney and is also living in the bungalow with Simon; Michael met Richard when they both worked in the Taxation Office in Sydney, in what they call 'a former life'. Chris Ash and his partner live next door, and various friends regularly drop in, including Kate McNamara from M Ward.

Kate's been writing more powerful poetry, and she brings drama and excitement to our encounters. Our friendship develops over cups of tea and conversations about poetry, astrology and magic. Whenever we're faced with a decision, we throw the coins to consult the I Ching, taking to heart the oracle's advice, enjoying the imagery, the ritual, the pondering. I love Kate's candid language and emotional volatility, and feel dull and slow beside her. When we delve into Chinese astrology, we discover that she was born in the year of the dragon, while I was born in the year of the ox. It seems that our personality traits are preordained.

Michael and I think it's destiny when Kate and Richard quickly form a romantic liaison. Richard is calm, ironic, easy to be with. He writes poetry, loves the Black Mountain poets and the Beats, and has a wry sense of humour – a perfect match for Kate. Like Michael, Richard is enthusiastic about drugs, and they have a long history of shared experiences, the source of many stories they recount in moods of great hilarity.

When all of us are together, poetry and music are our focus, and Simon's bungalow becomes a communal hub.

***

In January, I re-enrol in my course at ANU. Michael is happy to continue living in Canberra and is supportive of my plan to finish my degree, so we postpone our Jumping Creek dream and talk about finding a place to live locally. We want to stay close to the community in Hall; there's a sense of shared understanding in our friendship group.

Social occasions are informal and often spontaneous. When Chris and his partner get married, we all go to the ceremony, holding bouquets and enjoying the rituals. It's the height of summer, and we have picnics beneath the pine tree in the backyard. On hot nights we sit around in the kitchen with the doors and windows open, talking and listening to music.

But we're another band of 'displaced Romantics' and, for me, things aren't always as straightforward and relaxed as they appear. I still feel cut off from my experiences, as if my deeper being is detached and adrift. While I smile and seem to be part of what's happening, the connection is superficial. I sense that this detachment is a side effect of my medication, but anyone who's been depressed knows this state. I struggle with the burden of a grief I can't put a name to. A glass wall separates me from the people I care about.

My distress closes on me like a cell door. Michael feels this too. We talk about the green bell as something lost. It's as if sadness makes us blind, and we're feeling our way through the darkness, holding hands, sharing our heartache. We try to protect ourselves from the loss of light, from the loss of our encounter with ecstasy, but here, in the depths of melancholy, it's hard to hold on to the thought that 'this too shall pass'.

***

One warm night, I impetuously decide to take the plunge and smoke a joint.

We had one of Simon's famous vegetable curries for dinner and are now listening to Neil Young's *Harvest.* The doors are open to let the cooler air waft in. As usual, the table has collected pouches of Drum tobacco and cigarette papers, ashtrays erupting with butts, dirty coffee cups and, thanks to Simon, a basket of fruit. I like to imagine a time when Michael and I will have a place like this to ourselves, a place with a jar of flowers on the windowsill, an open fireplace, and our own kitchen table crowded with friends.

When the joint comes around to me, I take it and inhale, enjoying the aroma. After a few light drags, I relax into the warmth of the night, and the easy, loose conversation. A soft, benign high. I float in the music. It's a revelation. I begin to understand why people take to it so readily.

Later that night, Michael and I spread a rug under the pine tree. There's no moon, the air is soaked with the smell of resin, and we drift in the darkness, talking softly until gravity has its way and we're lying flat out on the ground, awed by the night and the fields of stars above us. I tell him that I understand his enthusiasm for marijuana, his 'magical herbal cigarette', and he squeezes my hand, pleased that we can now share this mood.

But a week or so later, after sharing a joint of hash with Michael, I discover that I can't move. We're alone together at Hall, sitting on a lounge in the area that doubles as living room and kitchen. It's dimly lit at the kitchen end, and music plays on the small stereo, drums beating, guitars wailing, as if there's been a catastrophe. My heart is palpitating wildly, my breathing is shallow and laboured, and the dread and fear that I associate with nightmares press down on my chest.

I'm nauseated and begin to hallucinate. The shadows in the room lurch towards me, swiftly retreat, then tilt again in my direction, playing with me, threatening. I look at my hands as they dissolve, a sickly flesh colour sinking into the blue of my jeans. My yellow sandshoes distort the shape of my feet, and the colour repels like vomit. It's hard to take a breath. Michael sees my distress and holds my hand until I come back to myself.

Only days later, I'm at a party with Michael in a student house. Rock and roll is pounding, lights are dimmed, and plates of finger food cover a table pushed into the corner of the lounge room. People are talking loudly over the music, and others are dancing. I'm on the periphery of the upbeat mood, drinking red wine and participating in the odd exchange with anyone passing by. Tense and restless, I'm not quite able to lose the feeling that I'm playing at being here and having fun.

I go in search of Michael and find him outside with a few others. As I approach, they look my way and go quiet. 'What's up?' I ask.

'We've got some speed,' Michael says. 'I'll come in later.'

'I want some,' I say. Feeling reckless, wanting to be part of the scene.

'Nah, you don't. Why don't you check out where Kate is?'

But I insist and, after some hesitation, Michael gives me a small white tablet that I quickly swallow. I'm ready for anything.

Back inside, we join a few people talking on a couch. Not long after, I feel an intense anxiety, and my nervous system surges with a sharp, unpleasant energy. I stand up, walk outside, can't stay still, go inside, start dancing. I can't speak, can't stop this electric charge that's singeing my nerves. I can't bear it; there's nothing I can do to stop it. I find a glass and drink water from the kitchen tap, go back into the lounge room to dance, having to move to release this bitter and nasty energy.

I know then and there that I'll never do anything like this to myself again. My medication may be interfering with the drugs' actions, or I may simply have a particular sensitivity. Whatever the reason, the drugs that many people are happily ingesting are poison to me. The one exception is the sought-after prescription drug Mandrax (methaqualone), a sedative-hypnotic that I've been prescribed to help me relax and sleep.

From the time Michael moved to Lennox House, the fact that I wasn't taking drugs opened up an uncomfortable space between us. It's clear now that they represent a significant gulf. He's on one side, wanting to escape from the ordinary world, escape from himself, and I'm on the other, desperately and earnestly trying to gain a foothold in everyday reality.

Ironically, for all the talk within the counterculture about being free and uninhibited, on the subject of drugs Michael and I are mute. I want to get away from hallucinatory worlds where my vision collapses around me, and sounds and voices play with my sense of reality, whereas Michael wants to lose himself in such experiences. I want to be connected to other people in a normal, everyday world, one in which days unfold predictably and nights lead to undisturbed sleep. I want to be able to walk in from the darkness, as in my fantasy, and sit at the table surrounded by light.

Michael has been enthralled by the romance of drugs, and he still gets into raves about their mind-expanding effects, but, with me, he talks about wanting to ease the pain, escape his despair, and get through stressful social situations. I think that now he needs drugs in order to bear the burden of himself. He speaks of wanting an ordinary life of small pleasures among people he calls 'real' – people who hold to what he sees as old-fashioned virtues such as honour, honesty and courage. He craves authentic, down-to-earth experiences with people. But while he knows that the drugs are a threat to everything he aspires to, this knowledge doesn't help alleviate his dependence on them.

In one of his letters from Caloola, Michael wrote, with underlining, ***'Drugs? Forget it!'*** He wrote in another letter, 'I've not had any ephedrine tablets since yesterday morning. Too much like taking drugs.' And once, in one of those moments when love makes all things seem possible, he whispered to me, 'I wouldn't swap you for all the poppies in Afghanistan.' He insists that love is his drug of choice, that he gets high on love, but I'm beginning to wonder if love will be enough.

Michael and I have no tolerance for ambiguity and conflict within our relationship, no understanding of how to negotiate anything that threatens our dream.

***

Although Michael feels isolated, in truth he has the support of other poets, both in Canberra and Sydney. He invites me to go with him to a dinner party at Geoff Page's house. Geoff is a Canberra poet and teacher whose first book of poetry was published two years ago. Michael and Geoff share the same publisher – and, more significantly, they share a dedication to their writing.

When Michael arrives to pick me up from my parents' house, something's wrong. He paces around the room and flings himself on my bed. He tells me that he doesn't want to go to the dinner. A social evening with other poets and writers will freak him out, he says. We talk for a while, and he changes his mind: it will be cool, he can handle it.

There are about eight people present, and the conversation ranges from politics to poetry. Geoff is a generous and hospitable host, and Michael's charm gets him through, though I sense he's tense and wired.

Afterwards, back in my room, he talks about his inhibitions, his anxiety, and his nervousness in social situations. He feels that drugs would have made the situation less nerve-wracking. As far as he's concerned, there's no doubt they help give him the confidence that he feels he needs to engage socially.

Another day, we visit David Campbell at The Run, his property near Queanbeyan. David is a poet of the same generation as Manning Clark and Patrick White, and he counts them among his friends. Michael is impressed by David's standing as a war hero who fought in the same region as Michael's father, earning the Distinguished Flying Cross for bravery. David's spent most of his life as a farmer and poet, living on a number of rural properties around Canberra, and many of his poems are inspired by his life on the land. A tall man, he has an open manner that invites trust. His face reminds me of the countryside, its granite and bare paddocks.

Guests are sitting around a low table, laughing softly and passing plates of food. Sunlight shines on grass that's wet from overnight rain, and there's a warm and loamy smell of soft earth. But best of all is Michael's happiness. David's very interested in his work, and Michael is animated and relaxed, talking about poetry and farming on the Monaro.

In the evening after our day at The Run, we head to Gus's cafe in Civic. We relive the afternoon as we eat our favourite toasted ham and tomato sandwiches and drink coffee. David Campbell is the ultimate 'Jack' figure for Michael, inspiring his visions of a life of poetry that has its roots in the land.

The contact with David also encourages Michael to think of his writing plans. He reckons that he has about three hundred poems from his time in M Ward, and he wants to keep the best of these for a collection that he decides to call *The Second Month of Spring.* He's also keen to write a history of the teamsters, those men who drove wagons drawn by teams of horses or donkeys, transporting goods and people overland through the bush. We make plans to travel around the country together, following their old routes. Logistics and practicalities don't bother us as we dream of searching for physical evidence of the past and sleeping under the stars.

When Michael is manic with ideas, full of plans for new projects, the future is irresistible. He's also considering writing about his father's navy regiment and their time in the South Pacific. And, Michael tells me, someone has invited him to teach his poetry at a university course in New Delhi, so we talk about me deferring my studies and us going to India together. Just the thought of taking off into a strange place and an unknown future is enough to give me hope that my depression will soon lift.

A few nights later, Michael saunters into my room exuding happiness and a kind of self-conscious confidence. He's written a few new poems and his mood is contagious. When he speaks of these poems, it's as if he hasn't a single doubt about his work. His eyes are a deeper blue, and his smile like a flame, flickering and leaping across his face. It's as if the world lies at his feet and everything is possible.

But the next day, this confidence has evaporated. He's plunged back into despair about his work and his feeling of isolation from other writers.

His attitude soon shifts again, and he reflects on the friendship and support that he's received from the writer and poet Rodney Hall, a particular friend and mentor since 1967. I first heard of Rodney in M Ward, where Michael spoke warmly about him. Now Michael tells me of a visit he once made to Rodney and his wife, Bet, when Michael was very ill – he'd collapsed at their door from what turned out to be pneumonia and pleurisy. Affectionately, Michael describes how they nursed him back to health.

When Rodney was the literary editor of *The Australian,* Michael sent him some poems. Rodney didn't publish any of this first selection of submissions, but he wrote a letter to Michael in which he discussed the work and asked him to send in more. Michael replied with a passionate rant against the lack of acceptance of his poetry but, in the end, he thanked Rodney effusively for his letter and resubmitted. This sudden change of mood is typical of Michael's mercurial style and his passionate involvement in his art. Rodney and Michael soon became friends, sharing a commitment to their work as poets and a deep love of music.

From what Michael tells me, the poetry scene in Sydney can be chaotic and cut-throat, but he revels in gossip of struggles and cliques. And he becomes animated when talking about the Sydney poet Robert Adamson, another friend, and how they spent whole days and nights together writing poetry, talking poetry, listening to Dylan and reading Rimbaud. He also talks about the poets Tom Shapcott and Geoffrey Dutton, describing how they've given him friendship and practical support, as well as the sort of encouragement that comes from people in your field having faith in your work.

But although Michael acknowledges the very real support he's been given, his profound sense of himself as an outsider seems entrenched in his psyche.

***

Lying in my room, ruminating on my life, I'm aware that our love is more ordinary now, less transcendent. I feel it in the simple things. The sight of Michael's hand holding a coffee mug, the way his voice changes when he talks of love, his habit of playing with the hair at the nape of my neck. More human and personal. I miss our ecstatic times inside the green bell, but I'm taking pleasure in Michael and the world around me.

I realise that the transcendent and the ordinary, imagination and reality, need each other. They're essentially one and the same thing; as Michael often says, 'Imagination is reality.' Michael is my true love and a human being. The green bell is a willow tree.

As I think about this, I feel that I'm a sailor at sea, finding my way home, the shore in sight. I'm leaving behind the extremities of madness, both the despair and the ecstasy.

***

One day in late January, eight of us go for a picnic on the banks of the Murrumbidgee. We spend a lazy afternoon sitting together in the sunshine with the river sparkling and casuarinas throwing shade over the fine sand. The feeling is light and loose; Michael is telling stories about Ludwig of Bavaria, and everyone is laughing. Time is boundless, the air is crisp, and the smell of the flowing water is earthy and close. We drink warm white wine from a cask and eat vegetable pie and salad from Tupperware while Chris plays his guitar. His collie dog, Issa, snores and twitches in her sleep, stretched out on the sand.

Later that day, Michael and I sit on the veranda at Lennox drinking coffee and eating cheese and biscuits. There's no one else around except for the possum that the residents call 'one-handed' because of his mangled leg. We place some food on the ground a short distance away and coax him to take it. He hops towards us, snatches it up and wobbles back to the plum tree. We watch him manoeuvre himself up the trunk, passing the food between his one hand and his feet as he climbs. Michael is stroking his wispy beard in the yellow light of the veranda, pondering the one-handed possum's predicament. We make up stories of his life's adventures until there's no food left and the possum has disappeared.

I head back to Hackett that night, and the next afternoon Michael and I go for a bushwalk at the back of the family house. We're strolling along a dirt track when we see a clump of yellow dandelions and stop to pick them. We pierce the stalks with our fingernails and make a chain. Placing the flowers ceremoniously in my hair, Michael jokes that I'm now officially a hippie.

We wander through the afternoon talking about Vincent van Gogh and the colour yellow, and my mind is soft with light – the yellow of the dandelions, the yellow in the conversation, the yellow in van Gogh's paintings – and it all comes together with the sunny day, the bush, the wattle, and the feeling of being with the man I love.

10

The Last Month of Summer, Early 1973

I'm woken from sleep by a soft knocking at the door of my room. I know it's Michael. He comes in wearing his old air force boots, and although I'm still in bed trying to drag myself to consciousness, I notice that the top flaps are undone. The curtains are closed, and my room is still gathered into itself, all soft contours and veiled light. Michael walks towards me smiling, bouncing across the floor with an excitement that alerts me to the possibility that this is no ordinary visit.

'Hello, you,' I say. I sit up, hold out my hand and pull him onto the bed. 'How's things?' I'm still thick with sleep, but I notice that he's looking at me differently, as if weighing me up in some way.

'I met up with Sally last night,' he says.

'Sally?'

'You know, Sally – the night nurse from M Ward. We bumped into each other at a party in Turner.'

'Oh, yeah, how's she going?'

'She's great. She asked about you.'

'Oh? What did you say?'

'I said you were as crazy as ever, just enjoying it more.'

'Yeah, right,' I say, smiling. 'So, how was the party?'

'Really cool. The most amazing thing happened. I'm really getting my health back, Pauls, I can really feel my strength coming back. Sally's got these Great Danes – huge, they take up the whole of the lounge room. We played with them, it was crazy...'

I'm now listening from a deeper region of myself. My mind becomes alert and clear. I see my room as if I'm looking in through the window, watching Michael and me sitting on my bed, the space around us chaotic. Clothes hang over chairs, papers are scattered over my desk, and I want to impose order, get things under control.

I hear footsteps in the hall of the house upstairs and muffled sounds of talking. I look back at Michael. 'Have you ever had a dog?' I ask. I'm not sure where this conversation is going, but I know that it's going somewhere.

'Yeah, I used to have a corgi, the Queen's dog, but that was a while ago. Had a cat too. Cats are mysterious and they purr, like this – *purrrr.*' Michael leans towards me, nuzzling my neck. 'I think I'm a cat *purrr* son.'

I laugh, pull his head closer and run my fingers through his hair. But I still sense a strange vibe. Michael is high, and I'm both confused and hyper-alert.

'So Sally has cats too?' I ask.

'No, just these Great Danes. Amazing dogs – gorgeous, aristocratic beings. You should've seen them.' Michael's eyes are shining. 'They're huge but really gentle. We were playing on the floor with them...' His expression is eager, expectant. 'The party was so cool – everyone was out of it. Sally and I were high. It was quite a night. We went back to her place afterwards, and I stayed the night with her. We slept together–'

'What do you mean?'

'Well ... we made love.'

I close my eyes against the pain in my heart. 'What does this mean?'

'Nothing, just that we were there together and–'

'But what does this mean for us?' I'm just not getting it.

'It doesn't make any difference to us. You're everything to me, Pauls. This doesn't affect us at all. It was nothing. Her husband was away, and it just happened.'

'Just like that,' I say. So many things just happen. Planes fall out of the sky. People die in their beds.

I listen to Michael's descriptions of how crazy the whole night had been with Sally. The tightness in my throat becomes more intense, so narrow it obstructs all the words I want to say. Words so huge they can't get through. Other words – small, light things – slip out instead. Their thin sounds float in the space between us like confetti. They say it's okay. They say I understand. That I can see he's happy. That it's great he feels so well. I smile, and I keep smiling. A mechanical clown at a fun fair.

When he walks towards the door to leave, I try to follow but find I can't make my legs move. It takes me a few seconds to get myself up, go outside and kiss Michael goodbye. He waves to me as he rides away on his Kawasaki. I stand in the doorway holding on to the frame, watching him through eyes of jealousy and loss as he disappears. My vision blurs. I couldn't be more shocked if he had hit me.

***

That evening, I stand in the hallway holding the phone to my ear, taking a deep breath. Michael has asked me how I am.

'I'm not so good,' I say. 'I feel terrible. Can't understand what's happened.'

'It's nothing,' he says. 'Nothing. Don't worry about it.'

'I don't want to see you tomorrow. I need to work things out.'

'That's cool.'

I'm silent. I can't speak. I hear through the receiver the sound of breathing.

'Okay then,' he says. 'See you in a while.'

'Michael,' I say urgently, before he can hang up, 'do you still love me?'

'Of course I do. I told you, what happened makes no difference to us.'

I don't believe him. 'Okay, good,' I say. 'See you soon.'

I'm burning with jealousy, the emotion that hates itself. My self-pity obsesses over my many failings. I'm not desirable, not exciting, not cool. Not interesting, beautiful, fun. Not part of the scene.

The next morning, I wake up to the sense that a catastrophe has occurred. Then I realise the commonplace nature of my heartbreak and turn to the wall, unable to face the day. I'm no longer Michael's beloved, and I miss him already. There's nothing left of my dream of him or my vision of the life we planned to share. I'm annulled and in pain. I don't know why – there's no point to it, no reason. Why do I need an exclusive love? My feelings are acid in my heart, my brain, corroding my sense of self. Unforgiving and unforgiven, the wound ulcerates. I am no longer the one.

I curl into the pain, hating the feelings that crush me, the weakness that takes me so far down that I'm unable to get up or speak. Another person speaks, functions in the world in my stead. I'm trapped inside the darkness again, head full of noise and abject silences.

There it is: I can't move, and I can't sit still.

***

A few days later, Michael and I decide to see a film in Civic. We don't talk about what happened. After the movie, sipping coffee in the outdoor section of Gus's cafe, we try to make conversation, but a deep pall has settled over us. I can't take for granted that I understand what he's saying, or that he understands what I'm saying, so I tread, step by careful step, through this new terrain, trying to establish a sense of where we're going. Michael is subdued, though, and I'm nervous and tense. When I look at him, my eyes lose focus, and he seems a long way away, unreachable.

'I'm working on *Going South,*' he tells me. 'It's shaping up as a sort of autobiographical prose work.'

'So it's about your life now? Are you writing about us?'

'Um, well, not really ... some bits, perhaps...'

'What have you said about us?' I ask, trying for a light, teasing tone. 'Is it all doom and gloom?'

'There's really not much about the present in it,' he says, flatly.

We both look sideways as a couple walks past, arm in arm. In the pause that follows, Michael puts his hand over mine. I pull away.

He strokes his beard as if nothing happened. I stir the coffee in my almost empty cup. A huge anchor drags through our deep silence. I feel something emerging, coming loose, but I don't know what it is.

'I don't think we should get married just yet,' I say. 'I think we need more time. To work things out.'

I see the shock on his face and realise what I've said.

'That's cool,' he says eventually.

He looks out across the street to the car park, his glasses glinting in the headlights of a passing van. I wait for him to look back at me. Instead, he reaches for his packet of cigarettes and takes one out. I pick up my tobacco and concentrate on rolling a plug, licking the edge of the paper and poking the strands in at each end with a match. Michael leans over and lights my cigarette before lighting his own. After inhaling deeply, he starts coughing – harsh, wrenching eruptions.

When they subside, he asks, 'Doing anything tomorrow?'

'Haven't any plans. What about you?'

'Not much.'

Another silence descends. We've both finished our coffee. The bill is on the table.

I sense myself falling. Nothing to hold on to, nothing to hold me together. In the chill air I try to breathe, but my chest has cramped as if I've just been told of a death.

I'm searching Michael's face for signs, but it's a pale mask. The man I know has disappeared. There's no part of him that I can reach. If I touch him now, he'll shrink from me. His eyes are distant, his mood restrained and cold.

I hadn't planned to postpone the wedding, hadn't even thought of it until the words came out. I've done something irrevocable.

'It's not long till the last bus,' I say. 'I guess I should be going.'

***

During the sleepless hours of the night, I realise that I've deceived myself. Immersed in the belief that our love was perfect, I've ignored the ambivalence, the questions, the loneliness that's crept into it since we left M Ward. Now I'm defeated by Michael's infidelity. I replay the moment he placed his hand over mine and I pulled away, and I'm gripped by regret. Maybe if I could have loved him in that moment, all would be well now between us.

The days pass. I can't concentrate, can't speak to people. The only person I want to talk to is Michael, but he can't be reached by phone. I obsess over the possibility that he wants to end our relationship. I retreat into my room under the house.

Then he rings me from a phone booth in Sydney. He talks about seeing friends there and going to parties; I respond with light chatter. Neither of us is able to confront our issues. I don't tell him that I'm spending the days and nights in anxious reflection. I don't say that I've realised my suggestion at the cafe was an attempt to force a way through to a conversation about our problems.

Buried in my room, I try to recover my faith in our future. I consider new and different possibilities for us – perhaps we could have an open relationship like de Beauvoir and Sartre. But I'm not convinced. I remember that in *The Prime of Life,* de Beauvoir admits to being deeply disturbed by Sartre's infidelity. After his affair with Olga Kosakiewicz, de Beauvoir asked herself if the whole of her happiness with him didn't depend on a gigantic lie. I know I'm not de Beauvoir but, like her, my response to Michael's infidelity is to question the very foundations of our love.

Without those foundations beneath me, I can't find the self-confidence to embrace a new dream. How can I once again be his beloved? I fixate on what he may be feeling, how he is, what he's doing. I wonder if he's as lost as I am, or if he's out having fun, feeling free and unconcerned about what's happened between us.

Our relationship has been undermined by madness and depression, damaged by drugs and 'free love'. It's been made fantastical by the illusions and delusions that we hold about ourselves and each other. Self-doubt and silence have created distances beyond the possibility of touch.

My mind races, thoughts attack me, and sometimes the noise returns. I know that my reaction is extreme, but I'm in the grip of something stronger than me. I fear I'll go mad again.

***

Michael rings me after he gets back from Sydney, and I drive Mum's car to see him at the Hall bungalow. My medication has been increased, and I'm sedated, less volatile. I'm determined to reach through to Michael. We sit in the kitchen, subdued and tentative with each other. We talk about his trip and, remembering the night I postponed our wedding, I put my hand over his as it lies between us on the table. I leave it there for a minute or so, but it feels awkward. I reach for my tobacco pouch and roll a cigarette. I smile. I'm friendly. I'm lost. We're tired. I drive home, headlights in my eyes.

Over the next week, we spend a couple of nights together at Hall with Richard, Kate and Simon. Michael and I are still quiet, nervous with each other, our speech laboured. Our talk is of anything but love, and he doesn't hold me. I don't hold him. He doesn't tell me what he's feeling; he talks about getting high at parties and being out of it. We don't mention what I said at Gus's cafe: it's as if it never happened. Yet it's built a wall between us – a wall I want to smash, but my anger at myself, at him, at the whole situation is buried in an unreachable vault. I'm in an emotional lockdown. Tranquillised.

Michael and Richard decide to visit a friend of Michael's in Melbourne, Mirka Mora. She's a Romanian Jewish artist, a survivor of the Holocaust, who emigrated from Paris to Melbourne in 1951, becoming famous for her art and her lively bohemian lifestyle. Mirka describes herself as a 'free spirit' who believes that you should never compromise – in art, in love, or in life. She's very like Michael, totally committed to her work, and she lives with spontaneity and a great sense of play. When Michael and Richard return from seeing her, they tell me of trips around the city and experiments with a variety of exotic drugs.

I still can't find a way through to Michael. Sometimes he's manic, but mostly he's aloof. We're in stasis; my words are stillborn and our conversations barren. One night, sitting across from each other in the living room at Hall, I become aware of him looking at me. I look at him. In the instant we see each other, we both look away, stung.

***

Early one morning as I'm dressing, I see that an envelope has been slipped under my door. Michael must have come to my room while I was asleep. I pick up the letter with a surge of hope. In happier times, he sometimes left affectionate messages and declarations of love under my door.

The envelope contains a copy of the Swinburne poem 'A Leave-Taking'. It's handwritten on lined white paper, and I recognise Michael's writing immediately, though it looks rushed. I read quickly.

Let us go hence, my songs she will not hear,
Let us go hence together without fear.
Keep silence now for singing time is over
And over all old things and all things dear.
Yea, though we sang as angels in her ear
She would not hear.

Let us give up, go down, she would not know
Let us go seaward as the great winds go
Full of blown sand and foam. What help is there?
There is no help, for all these things are so.
Though all the world were bitter as a tear
She would not hear.

It looks as if he copied it from memory – there are crossings out and rewritings, and many of the original lines have been omitted or altered. The word 'help' is written above the word 'hope', which he's struck through and corrected. I read the poem again and again. How has it come to this? *She would not hear.*

My confusion and incredulity increases, though the message is clear: our relationship is over.

I need to talk with him, to find out what's real. Am I a woman of stone? The moment that question occurs to me, I know the answer. In repressing my hurt and betrayal, I've repressed all other feelings, including love. Michael is acutely sensitive, and he knows me well. My emotional withdrawal has been worse than any words I could have said in anger and pain.

He's right. Our singing time is over.

I'm hopeless with remorse. By the time night comes, my mind is a threshing machine that I can't turn off. I feel that the world is about to turn on me again, pin me to the wall. The next day I stay in my room, only going upstairs to scavenge for food. Mum asks how I am as I hurry back down. My room is cold even though it's hot outside. I put on the electric heater, shivering and sweating, and try to make my mind deal with what's happened. It can only dictate orders: *Keep the door closed, keep everyone out, she would not hear. Let us go hence. What help is there?*

***

Two days pass and my mind settles. I know I have to see Michael, talk to him honestly about our relationship. I drive Mum's car out to Hall and step through the open door of the bungalow into the living room where Michael, Kate and Richard are sitting over cups of coffee. Michael jumps up and greets me with a smile and a generous, gangly hug as if nothing untoward has happened. He's in high spirits, seemingly happy and at ease with himself, and he claims to be getting stronger and healthier every day.

It's been a while since I've seen this playful Michael. He jokes around, showing off his muscles in a mock strongman pose. To demonstrate his strength, he picks me up and twirls me around the room, laughing and dancing. We fall into each other's arms in a spontaneous hug and, for that moment, it seems that we've rediscovered our love.

As we move away from each other, our eyes meet for a long moment. In that look, everything that's happened between us is acknowledged. It's a naked, disenchanted glimpse of our vulnerability, and an affirmation of what we shared, what we've been through together. An assertion of love and not-love. Together and separate. A key turning the world. We can now say the words we need to say. We've found each other again.

The weight of Michael's arm around my shoulders is a comfort as we sit on the lounge, drinking coffee and talking with the others. I've arrived just in time, they tell me: Michael is about to catch a plane to Sydney. He's going there to post bail for his dealer who's been busted. To me, this is a bitter disappointment. I'm determined to talk to him, work things out and assure him that I love him.

Hope is possible, but must be deferred. I'll have to wait until he comes back on Tuesday.

I breathe in the smell of soap, freshly washed clothes and cigarettes as I lean against Michael's chest. He is so familiar and so close; I bite the inside of my cheeks to stop myself collapsing into tears of frustration and exhaustion. His arm rests over me as if it belongs there. We're together again at last, and then suddenly it's time for him to go.

***

Late in the afternoon, a day after Michael's expected return from Sydney, Kate's car pulls into the driveway. I sense from her silence and intensity that something catastrophic has happened, and we go straight to my room.

'Michael has OD'd,' she tells me. 'He's in a hospital in Sydney. Unconscious.'

I sit on the edge of my bed. I can't speak.

'It looks bad,' Kate says. 'He's in a coma.'

'I have to see him.' I get to my feet and reach for my bag.

'He's not allowed visitors. His family are with him.'

That's all Kate knows. There's nothing to be done. I stand there, numb. The pressure in my chest turns off all feeling and sensation. Only my eyes move. They look at Kate, at the flowers on her faded tapestry jacket and at her thick sandy hair falling over her shoulders. They see her pale face and her blue eyes wild with shock. Once again, the axe is suspended above me.

***

A week passes. Michael remains in a coma. Whenever I shut my eyes, I see him lying in bed in a hospital room, his face like the Turin shroud. Each day in my room, I light a candle and I pray obsessively. *Please, God, please don't take him.*

Another week passes, and nothing changes. My life becomes very small, very precise. All the daily tasks and concerns are reduced to pieces of a jigsaw puzzle. This goes there, that fits here. One foot in front of the other. *Get up, get dressed, eat, drink, speak.* Each piece in its place.

Occasionally I go to lectures or sit at a library desk with books open in front of me. I talk myself through the days. But when night comes, there's only the image of Michael lying alone and unmoving in a hospital bed. I imagine visiting his room, lying next to him, stroking his face and gently waking him. In my own room, I light more candles, and I play Bob Dylan, Nina Simone and Vivaldi as if the music will wake him if I can only listen deeply enough. My own sleep is a fall into shadowy dreams that leave me in the morning with the familiar sensation of spider webs covering my face.

Another week passes. I'm standing on a cliff edge, about to fall. Feeling the updraft of vertigo, the lurch forward. The problem of how to get through the day, then the night, then the day again. At times I forget to shower and change my clothes. I'm desperate for a miracle. I imagine Michael walking through my door in his jeans and boots, his bag slung over his shoulder. 'G'day,' he says, smiling.

***

Somehow summer has turned into autumn, and Easter has arrived. On Good Friday, Kate and I go for a walk through a long plantation of pines and maples in Braddon. We can think of nothing but Michael.

It's a crisp day, and the ground is covered in a deep layer of autumn leaves. We wade through them, walking along in the shade, breathing in the smell of mulch and pine needles.

When we come to a clearing, Kate recites the opening lines of Michael's poem 'The hermit of green light': 'only the wind and a river know the way to his/hut in the woods, and sometimes only the wind'.

A bizarre, inexplicable energy explodes in us, and we start picking up piles of leaves and throwing them at each other and into the air. All the pent-up emotion of the previous weeks bursts through. A desperate manic wildness takes over. There are leaves in the air, on my face, and in the kaleidoscopic patterns of light in my eyes, gold and red, whirling and falling.

When I get home, I discover I've lost my engagement ring. My hand feels naked suddenly – my ring must have slipped off in the flurry of the leaf-throwing. Its loss seems a terrible omen. I take the steps two at a time and rush into the house, desperate to borrow Mum's car. I grab the keys off the telephone table and drive back to the park.

I rush around until I find the place where we'd thrown the leaves in the air. I kneel on the ground and brush the leaf mulch aside with my hands.

The smell of the earth and the mulch takes me back to the green bell. I drag my knees around like a crazed penitent until, after only minutes of looking, I see my ring lying among some leaves as if it was placed there. The small silver band is barely dusty.

I've found my ring. The impossible has happened.

Relief comes in enormous breaking waves. I'm kneeling, bent over the ground, crying, succumbing to the emotion, sobbing in hard loud bursts that leave me gasping for breath. Then a movement in a tree, maybe a bird, distracts me, and something shifts.

In the space of a breath, I feel Michael's presence. He's here with me, as close as my breathing, as familiar as the sense of coming home that I always have when he holds me. I smell his hair; I feel his love. Every cell in my body is singing. It's the strangest feeling, as if I'm surrounded by thousands of bees humming, buzzing, the air vibrating, drenched in sweet perfume. Michael is here with me, and I have my ring, my infinity ring, in my hand.

Then he's gone as suddenly as he came. But I know I will see him again. We'll be together, hold each other. I know it.

***

The Wednesday after Easter, I'm in the university cafeteria sitting at a table having a coffee and smoking a cigarette. The place is full of students back at uni after the break, lining up to get lunch, talking and laughing with each other. I don't see Simon approaching. Before I know it, he's there, sitting in front of me, his sandy hair brushing the rims of his glasses, his eyes pale. His posture is formal, upright.

I think of the afternoon with Kate on Good Friday, the leaves in the air, my lost ring. I look at Simon, and I know. I know that what I felt that day was Michael leaving this world, not coming back to it. His visit had not been a good omen after all. I stub out my cigarette and breathe in, suspended in time, waiting for the axe to fall.

Simon tells me that Michael died on Good Friday.

He tells me that the funeral has already been held.

***

A moment later, I'm no longer the person I was. I'm torn open and shut down all at once. It's possible that in some part of myself I knew this day would come, but I never knew it would feel like this. I consider finishing my coffee and decide against it. Simon is offering to drive me home, and it's raining, so I accept, grateful and relieved. I can't trust myself. The centre is everywhere. Anything could happen.

Simon concentrates on the road. His jaw is set forward against his grief. Both hands are on the wheel. In the silence between us, the windscreen wipers grind back and forth, erasing the droplets pounding the glass. The rhythm repeats in my head: *here/gone, here/gone.* The traffic crawls along. I think of a storm that rolled in towards the coast some years ago when I was at Narooma. The inky black of the sea, the purple sky, the wind as it dug at the trees on the shoreline. I hold myself firm on the seat of Simon's car. There's no shelter and nowhere to go. Michael won't be coming back from Sydney. *He's been cremated.* My mind is eclipsed by this thought. The totality of it.

I sense the storm coming closer. Somewhere in me, an energy is gathering that wants to tear to pieces everything in its path. We've stopped at a red light, and Simon is saying that Michael's mother will be coming to Canberra in a few days to collect his things.

I think of the hessian bag he carried his belongings in: his notebook and poems, letters, a few books, clothes, a little statue of the Infant of Prague. I know that when these treasures are gone, when my rage has laid itself waste and my pain is debris at the bottom of a cliff, the shoreline will have changed. When the storm is over, there will be claws where my hands are. After a death, you're not the same.

Michael is gone. *Cremated.* There is nothing to be done. No goodbye. No rituals to attend. No words to be said over his coffin. No leave-taking. No grave to visit. Gone.

11

Survival Is the Password

We die with the dying:
See, they depart, and we go with them.
We are born with the dead:
See, they return, and bring us with them.

–T.S. ELIOT, 'LITTLE GIDDING, FOUR QUARTETS'

A Canberra band is playing Daddy Cool's 'Eagle Rock', and the crowd on the dance floor is going wild. It's Friday night at the ANU Union Bar, and nobody's holding back. Red and yellow lights throb in the semi-darkness, and cigarette and marijuana smoke hangs in the air. I'm dancing in a crush of bodies to the pounding beat, stepping forward and back, holding my hands high. I've had a few drinks, the music's too loud to speak, to think, to care, and I intend to go home with the man I'm dancing with.

I've moved out of home, back into Lennox House. My life is a round of tutorials, waitressing and the Union Bar. Michael's beloved is gone. Hero lighting her candle and the ethereal Guinevere, they've gone too. I'm no longer even sure they existed. If they did, they could never have survived Michael's death. They were, in a way, his creation. In legend, Hero threw herself from her tower onto the rocks below and Guinevere fled to a convent. Neither outcome appeals to me. I want to live, and the person I've become is intent on doing that. She's fierce. She feels nothing. She's not going to cave in.

Julianne and I used to believe in an essential self: something unique, stable and enduring. We believed in Polonius's advice in *Hamlet:* 'This above all: to thine own self be true', and we held on to the idea that this self was ours by right as human beings. I saw it as the core of my existence, and I longed to reach it once and for all – but it always eluded me. Because the self is not what I'd imagined it to be.

Sometimes there's nothing inside. No self. I've felt that void and been that nonperson. Sometimes there's an iceberg where a self should be. Or a moth.

But since Michael's death, something has been rising within me, a surging, erratic energy that I'm riding like a wave, hoping I can make it to land, hoping I don't drown. Survival is the imperative, but waves are unpredictable. You might catch a wave that turns into a tsunami. Or a bitch wave – that's the kind I'm riding now. *She would not hear.* This is who I am. And being this person, being this bitch, makes me strong.

The coroner finds that Michael's death was caused by 'acute broncho-pneumonia and brain damage following a self-administered injection of an unknown substance'. My mind flees from the details of his death.

Sometimes, though, I see a fleeting image of Michael holding up a syringe and flicking a fingernail against the barrel. I almost feel something – but then the image is gone, and I'm on to the next thing. I am a million miles from him, from the green bell. The time I spent with Michael, our plans, his smile, have vanished from my life. I've become the unfeeling woman of Swinburne's poem that Michael slipped under my door. *Yea, though we sang as angels in her ear, she would not hear.* I could say that I've lost the capacity to feel, but it's truer to say that after he died I rejected the feelings that came. I would not let them in. They were robbers battering on my door, come to steal my life and sanity. After a while, the storm passed, the feelings stopped coming, and now I have none at all.

When thoughts of Michael circle me in the night, I take an intellectual approach. I reason that each person is ultimately responsible for themselves. But another voice objects that if we aren't responsible for one another, for the tangled lives that we live with other people, what's the point of it all? Still another voice insists that we live in hazard; we're subject to forces far greater than our own desires, and free will is a fiction.

But no matter how these thoughts obsess me, I know that there's no reasoning, no understanding – and no absolution. *She would not hear.*

***

The dimly lit room in the Hall bungalow smells of smoke, though the fire is low now and a draft blows in under the door. Our dinner plates are empty, and our conversation about Michael has become choppy. Thoughts are cut off in mid-sentence; it's impossible to complete an idea. Too much is unthinkable, and nothing can be said with any confidence. There's a sense of confusion, loose ends.

'It'd help if we knew why he ... or what he was...' says David.

'We'll never really know why,' I say.

'Some think that it was you,' Kate says.

Eyes turn on me.

'Who says that?' I ask mildly.

'People,' says Kate.

'You?'

'No. Not me. People in Sydney.'

I say nothing then. I know people think that I broke off my engagement to Michael and this was the reason he overdosed. I also know that regret is an emotion that turns back on itself, holds tight and will not let go. It has the logic of a steel trap. It will not release me from its jaws.

But I'm the bitch. I cope.

In 'Still Life', a poem dedicated to me, Michael wrote: 'we're much too close for any one/but death who watches & for god/who knows'. Death and God are a formidable duo, and I'm determined to have nothing to do with either of them – or with love. I'm obsessed by lines from a Wallace Stevens poem about a man, a woman and a blackbird. I feel that these lines are about love and death. From the time of his overdose in M Ward, a blackbird stood between Michael and me, creating an unholy trinity, an unsolvable mystery. Or a knot impossible to untie. People die for love, die of love, die without love, die in love, die in spite of love. I live in spite of death.

The wave I'm riding has brought me to land. I know that I'm not dead, though I live in cryonic suspension. Cold, frozen, hardly real. Kept awake at night by the noise, I can't look away from Michael's death, but I can't bear to see it either. I can't make amends; I can never fix things or make our lives good again. I can't make him feel better. I turn away because in the morning I have to get up and walk out into the day, into the naked sunlight. There's no way back from here.

I know I'll never love again the way I loved Michael. The passion and illusion of that type of surrender will not return. But I'm determined to survive. I float outside the stream of life, and I stay sane – if sanity is what this is. I'm Prufrock; I prepare a face to meet the faces that I meet, and I get through the days.

As the months pass, time loses its pace, becomes haphazard, forgetful. I want things to matter, but they don't. There's only the cold weight of each day, the misery of each night descending, the persistent sense of loss – and the vast distance between myself and others. I guess this is grief. If it is, its hallmark is absence. He's no longer here.

***

Somehow I've become mad again. I'm in Callan Park Mental Hospital in Sydney, and I'm trying to remember what happened.

I came down here with a man I was going out with. Stayed with some friends of his in Balmain and partied on without proper sleep for days. During a night spent in a park by myself, I lost connection with reality. As dawn broke over the harbour, I watched a motorboat slash the pink membrane on the surface of the water. The person I'd become split open. The bitch couldn't hold it together after all.

I was talking to people in a coffee shop about bees when an ambulance arrived and took me to an emergency ward. A doctor in a white coat gave me a hug, his hand holding my head hard to his chest. I could feel his heart beating. He told me that everything would be okay. A sharp pain caused by the pen in his top pocket pressing into my forehead brought me back to myself. For a few seconds the madness was contained. I could breathe. I was safe. The pain from the pen felt good.

Then I was brought here, to Callan Park, a large Victorianera institution. There seem to be hundreds of patients. My dorm is a long room with eight beds lined up, each bedhead against the wall. As I walk from my bed along the narrow room to the door, I smell stale menstrual blood. I turn away, grasp the crisscrossing bars at the windows and look out onto the grounds below. I'm locked inside a cage with the noise. At the door, there's a glassed-in booth for the staff. It's a severe institution, and I've been committed. They won't let me leave.

During the long stretch of afternoon, anxious minds obsess over old sorrows, and people are restless. I'm sitting on a bench in the huge dining room, talking to Ken, a nurse with long hair and eyes that are small behind the thick lens of his glasses. His manner is slow and casual, and though he looks heavy in his white uniform, he moves lightly among the patients. He calls me Hiawatha because my hair is in plaits and I'm wearing loose hospital pyjamas.

I feel I can ask Ken questions. Before this moment, I was pacing the cavernous but crowded spaces of the hospital, confused and tense. Now, Ken's explaining to me why the doctors won't let me leave, and he's talking about how I might change their minds. I've refused to sign the consent forms for ECT, and I'm desperate to leave. Ken tells me there will be an assessment in a few days. Doctors will decide then if I'm sane enough to be let out.

Ken explains it's important that I don't hear voices – I must tell the doctors that I've had a problem with critical thoughts, but I'll be fine if I can return to Canberra and continue on with my life. We practise saying this. Ken prompts me, running through the questions they'll ask about my life in Canberra and the side effects of the medication they've given me.

I'm determined to be sane at this meeting. Not mad, sad or bad. I will brush my hair and go in smiling. Say the right things.

Afterwards, I sit on a bench in the dining hall and make a vow to myself. I promise I'll never again have ECT or allow myself to be put into a mental hospital. I know that I have to be careful how I live – the wild life is not for me. I tell myself that I must find a way to deal with reality, with loss and grief, without breaking open. Bitch, slut, schizo, whatever, I'm going to be sane, and I'm going to live my life as a poem. For Julianne. For Michael. For myself. *Survival is the password.*

I soon find out that the assessment went well. I'm cleared to leave. The clerk at the desk gives me back my handbag and my clothes. I catch a taxi to Central Station and eventually find a bus to Canberra. I've been at Callan Park no more than a couple of weeks, and I'm ready to start again. I must mourn Michael and let him go. I must find a way to live with everything that's happened. I just don't know how.

***

When I first see the village of Captains Flat, it looks scarred and beaten, as if it suffered a disaster sometime in the past and never recovered. Huge slagheaps dominate the main street, and surrounding mountain ranges brood in the distance. It's hidden away in the Southern Tablelands, forty miles south of Canberra. I now live on its outskirts, in an old timber house set back from the road behind a row of coarse shrubs.

The Flat is not so much a town as a relic, what remains of a once-booming mining community. Dilapidated houses, many of them empty, sink into long grass behind collapsing fences, and a dusty general store sells what I need to keep me going. Downstream from the abandoned mine, the riverbanks are scorched bare of vegetation. The pub – which once boasted the longest bar in the country – is now mostly boarded off. Drinks are served in a dimly lit room with a dartboard hanging on the wall and boxes of dominos lined up on the windowsill. Thursday is darts night, and sometimes a meat raffle is held on a Friday. I'm an outsider in the town, but so is everyone who lives here, in their own way.

Tonight the moon is full and I've climbed to the top of the highest slagheap. Balanced on the rim of the mound and surrounded by shadows and outer space, I smoke a cigarette and my mind clears. The skeletons of a broken crane and other mining equipment lie around me at odd angles of collapse. I breathe in the acrid smell of damp slag and sulphur, and listen to the feral cats yowling as they mate in the darkness. The air in my nostrils and on my cheeks is as sharp as ice.

Earlier today I saw a dead wedge-tailed eagle. It was laid out on the footpath in front of the pub, wings spread to their full span, its head in profile and its cedar-brown eye glassy and fixed. I stopped and looked. The bird looked back at me with that one unseeing eye, its beak open in a silent death shriek. After a long moment, I stepped around it and continued on my way. Now, as I sit on top of the highest slagheap looking down at the town, I see in the foreground an image of the eagle. I look away but, against the dark sky I've turned towards, I see again the fixed shape of the dead bird, its wings outstretched in a parody of flight, its head bowed.

Everything about the slagheaps is stripped back. Dead tree trunks rise from stagnant ponds like claws reaching up from the underworld of the mines. In the daytime these ponds are fluorescent pink and orange with chemical seepage. Here in the moonlight they shine like mirrors. I feel at home here; I crave this landscape. I come here when the moon is bright so I can see my way to make the climb. It's too steep to clamber straight up – I have to angle my way across and around the side. I always stumble and slip, my feet dislodging rocks and gravel as I go. There's nothing to hold on to, and it's a long way down if you fall.

This place speaks to me of things that can't be said, of meanings that have to be endured alone. I sit here in some pre-verbal state of communion – not with Michael as himself, but with his death. I'm at one with the remote intimacy of the stars. I'm devoid of all feeling. These slagheaps are the landscape of my grief: austere, impersonal, cold. I belong here.

***

As I try to reach through to something real, I listen to music. The sound enters my heart and changes its rhythm, strengthens its pulse. I'm sure it even makes my blood richer, redder, as it enters my soul, bringing hope and life.

I'm obsessed with Rachmaninoff's *Piano Concerto Number 2 in C Minor.* I experience the love in the music and my love for the music, and each time there's a breakthrough to life. Julianne is with me. We're in the music. The world is playing.

Listening to this concerto, I come to understand madness in a new way. In one of its guises, madness is bondage to a reality that's insular and personal. It offers you the kind of truth you see when you're in pieces: a broken, defeated sort of truth. But Rachmaninoff's music allows me to see that madness is also a profound journey into the depths of the human soul, into my own soul.

As the intensity and momentum of the music peaks, I'm at the mercy of a power that can crush me. I'm wrestling with the dark angel, with the exquisite musculature of the music. I'm about to lose everything. But then the twin narratives of longing and loss enter the fray, weaving their energy through the melody. The encounter with the angel becomes a dance. We circle each other. Nothing is resolved, but everything is acknowledged. There is no danger now that I will fall into chaos. The truth of the music draws me back into life. The tragedy as well as the beauty of our hazardous existence is affirmed. I discover that others have fallen into the abyss – and then found their way back. People like Rachmaninoff.

When the music ends, I'm weak and trembling. I've lived through something profoundly disturbing, something that has put me in touch with the invisible, with voices that refuse to be silenced, with the darkest oceans of night. The emotional weight of the music leaves me humbled. I think of Rilke's poem 'The Man Watching':

> *If only we would let ourselves be dominated*
> *as things do by some immense storm,*
> *we would become strong too, and not need*
> *names.*

Rachmaninoff's concerto overpowers me like 'some immense storm', but it doesn't leave me feeling strong, only cleansed, somehow blessed. I accept that I know so little about life and how we all came to be, where we're going. Often after this music, I need to sleep.

***

Canberra has drawn me back, and I'm now living in a suburban red-brick house in Kingston. It's one of a row of houses that face a Greek Orthodox Church, just a short walk to the lake. The Maltese landlord leans on a stick and shuffles up the front steps to collect the rent every fortnight. He lived in the house for nearly thirty years and supplied local florists with flowers. One day he tells me that in spring the yard used to be full of daffodils, poppies, lilies, crocuses and hyacinths. Now there's just a jumble of broken wooden crates and weeds. And no matter the season, the house is always cold, even though I've hung a curtain to keep the heat in and painted the window frames bright yellow.

It's been two years since Michael died. I'm studying the final subject of my degree and working as a research assistant. I spend my days in a small, windowless cubicle in the National Library; I read journal articles and feel as if my life has reached a dead end. I was in a relationship but it broke down some time ago, so my social life now consists of long cups of tea with Kate McNamara and the occasional night at the union bar.

In the library cafe, I meet Leo, a PhD student who is forthright about politics and very sure of himself. One evening we have a picnic dinner at the Cotter River and, as darkness falls, we decide to go swimming. The cold water is breath-taking. I move against the current, watching the last of the light gleam and disappear into the depths. The dark shapes of the casuarinas mark the bank; high above, the evening star appears below the curve of a new moon. I feel warm inside my tingling skin, my body pushing against the river, the water's energy rushing through me.

Later that night, after a glass of wine, Leo and I are in bed together when my cat, Sappho, leaps from the wardrobe onto Leo's bare back. Leo roars with rage and tosses Sappho off the bed. I jump up and try to comfort her and placate Leo, who is yelling and pulling on his jeans while turning to the mirror, trying to see the scratches on his back. It's obvious he's hurt, so I start running around the house in search of bandaids, while Sappho, back on top of the wardrobe, glares at us and yowls.

I apologise frantically to Leo, but he's furious. He will not accept apologies and will not wait for me to put bandaids on his back. 'Fuck that cat! What the hell was it doing?' Making a threatening gesture at Sappho, he storms out of my house, slamming the door behind him. I don't expect to see him again.

I soothe my nerves by stroking Sappho, who by now is sitting comfortably on my lap by the heater, purring in her superior feline way. I'm still shocked. I lean close into the warmth of the heater for comfort until Sappho looks at me and meows, and the whole incident in the bedroom suddenly strikes me as funny. I start laughing, and before long I can't stop. I'm not sure whether I'm laughing or crying. Tears are rolling down my cheeks, and I'm convulsing so hard that I slip off the chair onto the floor.

Then I'm in no doubt that I'm sobbing, deep and gruelling surges of grief that bring with them searing memories of Michael.

Hours later, when there's nothing left in me, no memories and no tears, I make my way to bed. When Dad was exasperated with some aspect of our behaviour, he would urge us to 'wake up to ourselves'. Right now, in some essential way, I've woken up to myself. The hard truth of myself.

I open my eyes the next morning to the ringing of bells. The church across the road is celebrating a feast day, and I can hear cars massing outside in the rain. I lie in bed depleted and leaking tears, listening to the bells and the rain on the roof. Hours pass. I begin to move into the day. I sit at the table under the front window, sipping my coffee and watching the crowds huddle under umbrellas as they file out of the church. Droplets of rain coalesce and run in tendrils down the grey window, and I see that there's no truth in my life. I realise with a surge of pain that I've been sleepwalking through the days. I see myself at parties, drinking wine and laughing. Or sitting at my desk in the library under the fluorescent lights, busily taking notes. Apart from when I'm listening to music, I skate across the surface of my days, estranged from feelings and from people.

I'm no longer psychotic, but I'm not sane either. Madness threatens to hijack my thinking at any moment. Hypercritical thoughts attack my actions, my reactions. I'm anxious all the time. As I talk to people or cross a road, outrageous images flash through my mind: I'm tearing open my shirt and exposing my breasts, or falling into a crack that opens in the concrete. Once, as I stand on the footpath, I see myself stepping in front of a truck coming along the road. During a conversation, I imagine that the walls are about to fall on me. Constructing a sane personality that can function in the world is like trying to build a hut in the middle of a river. Sanity is an achievement, one that takes enormous effort, minute by minute.

I think of myself with Leo, going through the moves in the game of seduction, and I feel like a fraud. I remember Julianne's scorn for people who played roles that had no truth to them. 'They're faking it,' she used to say. And this is exactly what I've been doing for far too long. I have to endure the pain of my grief and loss; I have to learn to bear it. Otherwise my life will always be brittle and superficial. Although I enjoy the company of a few good friends, I have no genuine connections to anything beyond them. Kate's passion for life inspires me, but I'm still locked into the tight personality that I've constructed to get me through the days.

***

The week following Sappho's leap, I receive a postcard from Bill Beard, an old friend of Michael's. I met him last year at Umbi Gumbi, John and Wendy Blay's house near Bermagui. Bill is a wild man, a barefoot poet who spends his summers writing poetry and fire-watching in mountain ranges inland from the south coast. One inspired and hilarious night at Umbi Gumbi, his friends bestowed on him the nickname 'onion' – and, for me, it stuck, though I can't begin to say why. Now Bill's coming through Canberra and wants to meet up.

After dinner, he and I sit together on the lounge-room floor, and he tells me about his trip to the Flinders Ranges and the camel ride he took through the desert north of there. His eyes shine as he describes the beauty of the desert in the springtime and shows me poetry he wrote while he was there. He's living his life as a poem, and I must too.

Before the night is over, I've made up my mind to leave Canberra and travel to the Flinders Ranges. I can't wait – I want to be there by spring. The next day, I give notice that I'm leaving my job, withdraw from the last subject I need to complete my Arts degree, and buy a bus and train ticket to Adelaide. I visit my parents and, in the middle of the roast dinner my mother has cooked for me, I tell them that I'm leaving Canberra. We sip our wine, and they wish me well.

I have to cut all ties with this city. I plan to work in Adelaide during the winter and save enough money to take off to the desert by spring. I spend the next two weeks packing up my Canberra life, and at the end of May I leave the city for the last time. I know I'll never live there again.

***

I'm on the half-empty overland train, rattling through the night westwards towards the South Australian border. Passengers are asleep, lights are dim, but I'm wide awake. With my coat as a pillow, I curl up and read Patrick White's *Voss* under a dusty yellow light, transfixed by the magnetic intensity of the writing. I'm compelled to take this journey just as Voss was compelled to take his. He wanted to map a continent; I want to create a new life.

I have only one thought: to be in the desert in spring. See flowers bloom and excited birds gather at waterholes. I want to see it, but most of all I want to feel what it's like to be there. Stand under the sky, be dwarfed by the horizon. Feel the flowering plants break through the hard crust of earth, smell the crisp air, listen to birds calling up the dawn. I want to lie under the stars and open myself to mystery.

Images flicker through my mind as the night outside my window flashes by, taking my past with it. A future is rushing towards me. I want to be there when light breaks through the darkness, through my darkness.

***

In Adelaide, I open a wooden gate and see a house that reminds me of a child's drawing. The dusky pink wall at the front has a rectangular shape divided by two large windows either side of a green door. Above this wall is a triangular roof with dormer windows. I smell burning eucalyptus in the air and see smoke curling up from one of the tall chimneys. The grass is overgrown, and a cat is sitting on the porch washing itself. And, just like in a child's drawing, the angles are all slightly crooked, the fence is askew, the gate won't shut and the walls pitch to one side. It's one of North Adelaide's classic nineteenth-century homes, and in spite of the cracks and the peeling paintwork, it retains its old-world grace. My excitement mounts. I could live here.

A pregnant woman with a Madonna smile opens the door. She's holding a straw broom, and dust motes swirl around her in the sunlit hallway. Following her inside, I'm surprised by the space and the light, with high windows in the two front rooms, a wide hallway and tall ceilings. We walk down the hallway into shadows, past closed doors that the woman explains lead to the rooms of the other housemates. About ten people are living here, but right now they're out or at work. We move into light again as we walk into a long rectangular kitchen that has an open window above the sink and a table down the other side. By now I know that the woman's name is Diane Gerard and that her baby is due in a couple of months. I also know that I like her, I like this place, and I want to stay.

The room that becomes mine in the house on Mann Terrace, North Adelaide, is one of two that occupy the attic, on the left at the top of a narrow staircase. The ceiling is steeply pitched, sloping along the length of the space, forcing me to stoop on one side. An east-facing dormer window looks out over parkland.

The room is empty except for a mattress on a faded rug, so I need to get to work. I paint the walls and ceiling white and the trimmings green, buy an old chest of drawers and a cane chair from a second-hand shop down the road, and find a wall vase that I fill with trailing ivy. With a candle and my small tape deck placed on an upturned wooden box next to the mattress, and my clothes stashed away in drawers, I settle in quickly. I'm ready to create a life for myself.

Adelaide is exhilarating, liberating. Arriving in a place you've never been before is freeing in a way I've never experienced. I'm a stranger among strangers. The good girl, the mad girl, the beloved, the bitch are in the past, and the past is gone. No one here knows those people; here, I can be anyone. This idea is quietly astounding. No one knows my name. I have no idea who I'll become. But for now, I can say, 'I am.'

Everything I see, I'm seeing for the first time, and every street corner poses a question of which direction to take. Adelaide is a small city with remnants of its country town origins still recognisable in its buildings, parks and especially its cafes. On my first morning, when I order tea and toast in a cafe, I'm brought a large teapot covered with a woollen cosy, a jug of milk, jars of vegemite and marmalade, butter in a dish, and two slices of toast each an inch thick. 'Let me know if you want a top-up on the tea, love,' the waitress says over her shoulder as she walks back to the counter.

***

A few weeks after I arrive, I put my name down at an employment agency. Within days they let me know about a job in research at One to One Films, a women's film unit sponsored by the South Australian Film Corporation. When I'm offered the job, I panic. It's a six-month contract, and I'm supposed to be leaving for the desert in early spring.

I spend a sleepless night trying to decide what to do. As dawn breaks, I sit at my dormer window watching the sky pale into pastel colours over the dark shapes of parkland trees. I sense that the spring I'm craving is happening within me, here in this footloose household of nomads. I feel invigorated and buoyant, as if I've been underground for a long time and have just burst through into light and air. I decide I'll take the job, spend the spring in Adelaide and go to the desert another time.

I head into the city to get work clothes. In a small boutique on Rundle Street, a woman in a sleek green skirt offers to help me find what I'm looking for. I tell her that I'm starting a new job on Monday. She looks me up and down, registers that I have no dress sense at all, and selects a range of skirts and tops for me to try on. When I emerge from the dressing room in a green skirt like hers and a black fitted top, she nods her approval. I look at myself in the mirror – all I need to do is clip my hair up, and I'll be ready to start.

The idea of working with feminists to make films about women excites me. I imagine delving into issues that affect us and creating films that make a difference. It's just the sort of challenge I want to take on.

***

My housemates are becoming important to me. They're an eclectic group, a tribe of travellers from England,

Canada and New Zealand, with a couple of Australians thrown in. They're living the dream of the decade with all its ideals and contradictions – and they've made space in their lives for me.

The house buzzes with energy. It rocks to loud music, gets high on dope, trips on acid, dances all night and goes quiet in the early mornings. It overflows with the sounds of Bob Dylan; J.J. Cale; Bob Marley; Jefferson Airplane; Crosby, Stills, Nash & Young; and Fairport Convention. And it empties for occasional excursions to the corner pub or for picnics in the Adelaide Hills. It's a house where people hang around the kitchen to gossip and cook, and children wear their dress-ups all the time. People fall in love here, break up, cook together, eat together, go to work, play, go to the market. People are light-hearted, and they take care of one another.

No one has expectations of how you should behave, what you should say, how you should be. I can relax with the group, talk or not talk, withdraw to my inner world or take part in what's happening. It's easy to move in and out of conversations. I enjoy a gentle high when I'm with people who are stoned; they are loose, the conversation is loose, and my anxiety eases, floats away. I shared a joint one night but the effect wasn't relaxing, so now whenever I'm offered one I pass it on, and no one cares or comments. But they do think it's hilarious when I iron my jeans.

This is the sort of life that Michael would have relished. The mutable moods, the anarchic way it all functions, the spontaneous craziness. I sometimes feel his presence here. The other day, I was so sure he walked past as I climbed the stairs to my attic room, I reached out to touch him. And as a group of us sat around the lounge room listening to music, I glanced up and saw Michael sitting on the floor, looking at an album cover.

I feel my grief for Julianne and Michael in a new way. In Canberra it was an icy absence that I carried in my chest, but in this hippie household I experience the pain of it – and a whole range of emotions, both painful and pleasurable, emerge as well. I hold on to the toughness I discovered after Michael died. I listen to the lyrics of a Dylan song and think to myself, *The noise should not think it can bury me; madness should not think it can destroy me. I will have a life.*

Through the nights filled with music and the days sitting in the shade under fruit trees in the backyard, Julianne and Michael are here, inspiring me to live life as a poem. I remember a line from T.S. Eliot's poem 'Little Gidding' and think to myself: *See, the dead return and bring me with them.* Michael was right, 'survival *is* the password'. And Rilke was right to insist that endurance is all. And when Julianne said that the world is music playing, she was telling me something that becomes more and more significant to me as time passes. I'm coming to believe that the essentials of a good life are kindness and music.

I'm living my life day to day. I have no plans, no idea where I'm going. I wake up each morning to a new day and throw myself into its dramas and poetry. I discover a happiness that has roots in dark places but grows towards the sun. A lightness, a warmth – and the wish that Julianne and Michael were alive and could share these generous and uncomplicated days. It's not that there's no pain or confusion; what is different is the sense that I'm connected to other people and to myself. I'm no longer standing outside in the darkness; life has let me come inside.

After seven months at Mann Terrace, at the height of summer and with the sun in my eyes, I have a car accident – and am very nearly killed.

12

The Quest

My car is an orange beach buggy, a folly of mine, a flimsy vehicle I named Zelda. My accident happens when another car slams into Zelda just a couple of feet behind the driver's seat – behind me. I'm only a second away from being a direct hit. The car rolls three times. Luckily, the buggy has a strong roll bar, and I have a harness seatbelt.

The emergency room is a blur, moving into my field of vision then disappearing as I lose consciousness. It appears that I'm paralysed from the waist down. A specialist is called. He examines me – then, without warning, he hits me across the face. My body goes into a violent spasm that lasts for several minutes. Feeling returns to my legs. The doctor explains that I had shock paralysis, a temporary condition, and that being hit has brought me out of it. My injuries are minor, and I'll be home from hospital in a few days. My friends from Mann Terrace visit with flowers and freshly baked caramel slices. I'm dazed and happy to have survived. Amazed at my luck.

The next morning, Sean Mangan, the Irish-Canadian resident who occupies the attic room next to mine, comes in to visit on his own. I've had a crush on

Sean for some time, but I've been particularly aware of it since I listened to him sing one night as we sat around the kitchen table. His voice is strong and deep, and after I heard him sing old Irish ballads of love and parting, I was hooked.

Now, sitting next to my hospital bed and looking serious, Sean tells me that he loves me. He realised it when he heard about my accident. He knew he didn't want to live his life without me.

So much to take in. Perhaps I'm delirious. Or dreaming.

Three months later, we fly away together on April Fools' Day, our main destinations being Ireland and Greece. But, as we say, anything could happen. Taxiing down the tarmac, I put on my headphones and, just as we lift off into the air, into our future, The Eagles begin singing 'Take It to the Limit'. I'm ready for whatever comes.

On a hot night in Athens, we rest on the stone steps of the Parthenon and watch a blood moon break free of the horizon and rise like a god in the brilliant sky. We plan our next move. We've travelled around Ireland and lived in a clifftop room on the island of Santorini, and now we're running out of money. The idea of travelling to Toronto and finding work there comes up.

'Might be tricky for me to get a job without a visa,' I say.

'That's a thought.' Sean pauses for a moment, then says, 'We probably should get married. That'd sort it.'

'Married!?'

'Yeah. What do you think?'

'Okay,' I say, amazed.

Back at our hotel, we share our news with the night porter.

'We're going to get married,' I say.

'Ah,' he says, shaking his head. *'Finita la musica!'*

The reservations I once had about marriage haven't crossed my mind. I care only about the journey with Sean, the momentum. The romantic in me has won out. That and the blood red moon rising behind the pillars of the Parthenon, the yowling of wild cats in the alleys below, and Sean's hand holding mine.

***

Our wedding is just as we want it: low-key, no fuss. A couple of months after arriving in Toronto, we make our vows in the company of Sean's parents, his sister and brother-in-law in the lounge room of the celebrant's suburban house. My wedding outfit is a burnt-orange crêpe dress from the 1920s that I found in a country op shop, and Sean wears a white gypsy shirt with billowing sleeves that I made for the occasion. We pledge our love beneath a huge painting of the Rock of Gibraltar, then have lunch at a Holiday

Inn, getting tipsy as we toast our future with champagne and Sean's father bestows on us an Irish blessing.

Falling in love is one thing; making a life together is something else. I'm living on the edge of a precipice, suffering vertigo, every minute gulping air, about to fall. My jaw aches from clenching my teeth, from holding the smile. I've discovered that I can survive the loss of people I love, but I don't know if I can survive love. To be so close, so exposed. Love is excruciating. Maybe impossible. I can't trust love. I can't trust anything. I feel I'm about to fall into the mad pit and won't be able to get out. Working, sharing a house with friends, travelling around Ontario. All the time, holding on to sanity with broken hands.

Then, in the spring of 1979, Sean and I return to Australia and settle at Kangarilla in the Adelaide Hills. I'm starting life all over again. My mother sends a package of housewarming presents that include thirteen linen tea towels from her cupboard, all freshly ironed and smelling of eucalyptus. I love being in the hills, and I breathe deeply the perfume of freesias on the roadside, wattles in flower along the track to our house, creamy jonquils massed in the garden. The sunlight in the Adelaide Hills is cleansing; the night sky is astounding. It's so good to be home.

We sit on the veranda of our rented cottage and look out across rows of grape vines to the hills and sky beyond. Sometimes at night I stand on the veranda in the darkness and peer through the window at our lounge room. I see the roaring fire in the grate, a coloured crochet blanket hanging over the back of a chair, a rug on the floor, and Sean turned towards the fire playing his guitar. I'm on the outside looking in, but now I can walk in the door and pull up a chair. The room filled with light is in my own house.

Nine months later, our red-skinned, screaming daughter is placed in my arms. Rowan Kathleen becomes the pivot of my life. No one told me it would be like this – her existence marks the most radical shift in my life, in myself. I look at her, and I feel strong. I am a lioness with her cub; I would do anything for her, and the thing is, I *could* do anything for her. She has changed everything. I think of an image from a Francis Webb poem: 'To blown straw was given/All the fullness of heaven.'

***

Four years later, I'm asking myself what's happened to Sean and me, to our marriage. We are two people who shared a life for ten years but have now stopped sharing a life. As I learn to be alone, I try to find some meaning in the time we spent together. I want to understand what it leaves me with, what remains. I stand on Semaphore Beach, and I feel empty, like nothing, like night.

One morning, Rowan tells me that she dreamed she took a big bite out of a nice red apple and found a horrible fat worm inside. She feels cheated and cross, and will not eat her breakfast.

Not long after, I pack up our belongings in our Toyota station wagon. We drive to Melbourne on a straight route along the highway, trying to make it in one day. Rowan and I are soon living in an inner suburb just a couple of kilometres from my sister Annie and her family.

Late one afternoon, Rowan and I go walking around Merri Creek, just down the hill from our place. The light is fading but it feels wild among the trees, and we don't want to leave.

As the sun sets, a full moon rises, and magic is in the air. Rowan throws a stone into the reflection of the moon on the surface of the creek. As the stone lands, the moon's reflection breaks into thousands of fragments, rippling and shining in the darkness. A river of stars among the trees.

Gradually the moon re-forms, and Rowan laughs and throws another stone at it, watching as it disintegrates again. She continues to throw stones at the reflection, and each time as it re-forms, she calls out, excited, 'It's coming back!' The silver plate of the moon, shattering and then re-forming, and shattering again.

We're eating wild fennel seeds. I see the flash of light on a bird's wing, and hear birds calling and twittering. My daughter says, 'Mum, the trees are filled to the brim with birds.' And I am filled to the brim with love.

Rowan and the world. Like the moon, I break. And I re-form.

***

Survival isn't enough. To endure isn't everything. I want more. I'm on a quest to be healed, and my quest-ion is: Can I free myself of madness?

With immense effort, I can be sane on the outside. When required, I can arrange my face, walk through the door and come out the other side smiling. I can play that role but, on the inside, the madness attacks the person I'm trying to become. The strain and stress of keeping the sane, smiling woman separate from the mad noise is like fighting from the trenches, every day trying to keep the enemy at bay. It's not the way I want to live.

I've been meditating for about four years now, ever since Rowan was two years old. A friend told me about a meditation group he was part of and the healing effects he experienced following his initiation into it. An image formed in my mind of a mandala, of wholeness, of being healed. I started going to the meditation sessions, then chanting and meditating in private as well, and later I placed a photo of the guru on my desk.

So I go to India. To reconcile the dualities of madness and sanity. To open myself to grace. To pray.

Dawn is breaking as the bus stops outside the front gate of the ashram. Through the windows I glimpse a large gong suspended from a metal frame at the side of high ornamental gates and a stone wall. A woman in a sari is kneeling on the ground in the semi-darkness and drawing a mandala on the path, and people are gathering around the bus. Rowan awakens quickly, excited. As she picks up her small backpack, and I collect my larger one, a man in a *lungi* beats the gong with a mallet. I smell incense in the air. We stand there, surrounded by the sound of the gong and the animated voices of men organising the luggage.

The sky is luminous behind the whitewashed ashram buildings, and in the small trees along the road, birds are singing. Hindus believe that the world was created with the sound of a gong. I imagine that the world we're about to enter has come into existence at this very moment just for us.

Some days later, I enter the ashram temple for a special intensive meditation session. The marble floor is smooth and cool beneath my feet. The long hall with its high ceiling and wide-open windows is filled with rows of people sitting on floor cushions. Incense floats in the air like veils of gauze. I breathe in, absorbing the atmosphere of excitement and anticipation. Just as the *bhajan* group begins the chant, I find a place for myself.

Before long I'm lost in the music. The resonance of the sacred words, *om nama shivaya, om nama shivaya,* opens my mind and drowns out the mad thoughts. As hundreds of us descend into meditation, the chanting ceases and a hush descends on the temple. Time opens into a silence that's filled with grace and love, and I give thanks for my life. As the guru passes by me, she brushes my head with peacock feathers. I lean towards her to touch the hem of her robe, and my heart is pounding, my face is wet with tears. I feel like the woman in the Gospel who said within herself as Jesus passed by, 'If I may but touch the hem of his garment, I shall be whole.'

Rowan and I settle easily into life at the ashram and stay there for two months. My day starts at three-thirty when I pull myself out of sleep and slip into the temple for chanting and meditation. Afterwards, as dawn breaks, I stand in front of an outdoor fire sipping hot chai under a muslin sky. As I warm my hands on my cup, I watch the leaping flames light up the faces of the people around me, catching the white of their teeth, the gleam of their eyes. I breathe in the dawn, the gentleness of the light, its stillness and its promise.

Later in the morning, Rowan joins the other children at the school where they're told stories from the *Bhagavad Gita,* and they draw mandalas and pictures of Hindu deities. In the afternoons we join a group of parents and children in the lush ashram garden to do our *seva,* the work that's our contribution to the ashram community. We water the plants – and sometimes the children – and together play games as we take brooms to the crisscrossing paths, ensuring that not one leaf remains on the smooth stones, not one weed in the garden beds.

I feel immersed in a spiritual reality that gives substance and meaning to my daily life. I honour the image of the guru as the teacher who can help me connect more deeply to this reality, and free myself from thoughts and feelings I can't control. I believe that if I just keep meditating, I'll be healed.

***

On our return from India, Rowan and I start creating a life in Melbourne. She goes to the same school as her cousins, and we develop a weekly habit of having a spaghetti dinner at Bakers Cafe on Brunswick Street. During the day, I work part-time cleaning houses and gardening, and attend classes in Naturopathy at the Southern School of Natural Therapies. I continue to meditate, and I embrace the teachings of the guru with even greater devotion.

At times I'm able to connect with a state of being that transcends the personality I create to get me through the day. I think of this state as pure consciousness, not unlike the Buddhist understanding of emptiness: a seamless reality that pervades everything and is everything. It's the immanence of the mystics, the love of Rumi, the inspiration of the poets. It's the music that Julianne discovered: the music that lives in us and is the world playing. It's the 'somewhere else' that Michael's poems came from. When I'm able to immerse myself in this reality, it becomes the ground of my being, linking me to an inner sense of self.

But I haven't been healed; there's been no miracle. While I've added a spiritual dimension to my life, my daily struggle with hypercritical thoughts and a hypersensitivity to other people's energy continues. It makes being with people a constant strain, if not impossible. I'm exhausted from dealing with feelings of being attacked and undermined as I try to hold my life together. My mind twists and turns and will not let me rest, but I hold on to the hope that meditation will eventually free me of tormenting thoughts.

Eighteen months after returning from India, I discover that my guru's guru, the teacher who brought his sect to the West, has been involved in sexual exploits with female members of his circle and sexual abuse of young girls. I'm devastated. A number of people from the group, including a former female swami who is now a friend, corroborate the stories that are circulating.

My faith in the guru, and in the concept of a guru, collapses. I stop attending meditation and chanting sessions. I feel like I felt when I lost my Catholic faith – I've lost the ground beneath my feet.

***

My breakdown this time is less violent and more gradual. As I become aware that I'm losing touch with reality, I recognise that I need professional help. I can't tolerate the thought of seeing a psychiatrist, but I find a psychotherapist who's willing to take me on as a client. He is eclectic in his practices, drawing on the works of Sigmund Freud, Carl Jung, Melanie Klein, Fritz Perls, existential humanist philosophers and others. When I'm acutely psychotic, he administers lemon juice to my eyes, a technique he observed being used in the Philippines for people suffering delusions and disorientation. The effect is immediate – it briefly shocks the brain out of psychosis, giving me some time to process the thoughts that overwhelm me.

Therapy with this psychologist involves a long journey through my inner world. I explore my delusions and illusions, trying to find their meanings and learn how to manage them. Throughout, I struggle with noise, the mind's incessant talking at me, and mad voices and images. I can't turn the madness off. But, in time, I learn to talk back to it, even converse with it, and sometimes I just write it out of me, like lancing a boil, to ease the pressure in my head. At other times, I walk hard and fast around Merri Creek, or curl up in bed with the curtains closed.

During the day, I'm aware only of the need to be functional by the time Rowan comes home from school. Around two-thirty, I focus on physical activities in an effort to get my mind to slow down. When Rowan arrives an hour or so later, I become the mother: I walk through the door leaving the mad woman behind me. I smile; I give Rowan a hug. The mother knows what to do. She takes Rowan shopping, does the washing up, then cooks dinner while Rowan reads books and does her homework.

Together we watch *Hey Dad..!* and *A Country Practice.* For me the tension is almost unbearable – just to keep my mind on track, hold the mother together. Bedtime is the hardest because Rowan has trouble getting to sleep. The mother tells stories, massages her legs, slowly counts backwards from a hundred. But I can't hold the mother together for much longer. I walk out of Ro's room, leaving the door ajar. Hoping she'll sleep.

I worry about how my mental state is affecting her. She's now eight years old and always has her nose in a book. One day as I drive up the road to our place, I see her coming home from school, her bag on her back and a book open in her hand, reading as she walks along the street. She seems so contained, so self-sufficient. But another day while looking through my books, I come across a torn piece of paper wedged between two pages. Written on it in child's writing is: 'Hullo. Is anyone there? Is there anyone I can talk to?'

I know something of what it means for Rowan to have me for a mother. I know there are good times. We have stories, songs, wild and playful adventures, cuddles and games. And we have a dog, a black kelpie cross named Pippa. When we brought Pippa home, Rowan said, 'We're a real family now.'

Sometimes my daughter goes to Adelaide for holidays with Sean and comes back with new songs she's learned. Once she came back with a guitar that she immediately set about learning to play.

I also know that life can be very hard for Rowan. She endures long stretches of loneliness. Through these times, she looks after herself; she reads books and tells herself stories. What she endures beyond the loneliness, I can only guess.

There's one imperative in my life: to stay sane for the times that Rowan is with me. When I can't hold it together, she goes to Sydney and stays with my sister Irene, a Brigidine nun who's now the principal of a primary school. More regularly, Rowan stays with Annie, who is a constant support in our lives. I don't know what I'd do without Annie and Irene – their ongoing generosity, their sensitivity and care. This isn't just a figure of speech: I literally don't know what I'd do without their help. I worry that I'll fall off the cliff and lose Rowan. Become homeless, go to prison, lose my life.

I keep working with the psychotherapist on my delusions and hallucinations. The more I examine them and tell their stories, the more I'm able to integrate them with my emotions and with language. It's a long and painful task to bring sanity into the chaos, to moderate the irrational with the rational. Madness is cruel, and sometimes I have no idea what sanity is or what it feels like. It's essential to have the support of a professional who knows the pitfalls of the journey and can handle psychotic imagery.

While I'm immersed in psychotherapy, books become another lifeline. My eyes don't leave the pages of Martin Buber's *I and Thou* as my mind is opened to the concepts of dialogue and the I–Thou relationship. He believes that this open and responsive relationship is the existential reality through which the self comes into being – in other words, the self isn't something you're born with; it's created through relationships with others.

I realise that my self isn't an object, an entity, but rather a process, always in flux. My self is a mutable flow of energy, my inner world intersecting with the world around me – adapting, choosing, responding, initiating. Creating a fluctuating pattern that I recognise as being me. My identity is an interplay between being and becoming, stillness and movement, opening and closing.

I'm venturing into new territory. I read Paul Tillich's *The Courage to Be* and discover ideas about anxiety, non-being and being, and the importance of having the courage to bear these states. I see that the pain of my existence is an experience that belongs to me as a human being. Suffering is part of the deal. I remember Michael saying that the only true things are love and suffering. I take deep breaths and learn to endure.

Viktor Frankl's *Man's Search for Meaning* changes me too. Frankl was a psychiatrist in Vienna before being interned in Auschwitz and later Dachau by the Nazis. His primary question was: When faced with unimaginable suffering, why do people not commit suicide? Frankl quotes Nietzsche, 'He who has a *why* to live can bear with almost any *how*.' He concerns himself with how people make larger sense of apparently senseless suffering, how they find meaning. I read his book from cover to cover in a few hours, and then I read it again and take notes.

Inspired by these writers, I enrol in a postgraduate diploma in Psychoanalytic Studies. I study the work of psychoanalysts such as Sigmund Freud, Karl Jung, Melanie Klein and Julia Kristeva. This study brings to my experience of therapy a structure and a discipline that, while not as inspiring as the existentialists I'm reading, gives me a sense of the complexity of the human psyche. I see how I can make choices that affect both the unconscious and conscious dimensions of my mind. I read every theory about madness that I can find, and I try to understand my life's trajectory.

***

During a psychotherapy session, I remember an original trauma of temporarily losing my mother when I was very young. When I ask Mum about it now, she tells me that I was hospitalised for six weeks just before my second birthday – I'd contracted measles, mumps and chicken pox simultaneously. I have memory fragments from that time; one involves an unbearable sensation of air being blown on my skin from a fan at the end of my bed. Even now I can see the ward: the arrangement of the other children's cots, and the door through which the nurses came and went.

I also remember the day my mother arrived to take me home. She was carrying a baby in a pouch on her chest. The shock of her holding a baby. Me. Not me.

When I ask Mum if she visited me, she says, 'We knew you were being well looked after.' I was at the Royal Alexandra Hospital for Children, and she had no doubt that visiting me wouldn't serve any purpose and would probably upset me. There were also practical reasons: the hospital was a long way from where my family lived, and she was heavily pregnant with her fourth child and had two other young kids to care for. She gave birth to my younger brother while I was in hospital.

At the time, there was very little understanding of the depth and importance of a child's attachment to its mother. I know that Mum would never have left me alone if she'd thought for a second that it would cause me the grief it did.

In this original experience of separation from my mother, I lost the confidence that the presence of a primary carer gives a child. Even though Mum came back, another baby was there in her arms, not me. My child self couldn't integrate this experience of loss into my precarious and unformed sense of self. For six weeks, I was cut off from everything familiar, and I was ill with delirium and physical pain. When Mum left me at the hospital, my whole world disappeared and, with it, my self. When it was time for her to bring me home, she had another baby there; I never recovered my place in her arms.

I now believe that this early trauma is the origin of my extreme response to loss and the threat of loss. In my breakdowns, I revert to the hallucinatory state and psychological disintegration that I experienced as a twenty-three month old. This experience is at the core of the anxiety that I carried as a child, and of the madness that first erupted into my life with Julianne's death and then again when Michael died.

***

Although I pledge myself to sanity, at times during psychotherapy the madness spills out again, but with enduring support from my family and friends, good professional help and good luck, I'm able to avoid hospitalisation.

But while I'm immensely grateful for the healing and insight that psychotherapy brings me, it hasn't been an ultimate cure. I've come to the view that, very possibly, such a cure doesn't exist. Still, I'm not ready to give up, and I'm stronger now. I can manage the madness and develop a more cohesive and fluid pattern of energy that I can depend on to be myself in the world. I'm building a hut in the middle of the river where I can rest.

It's my fiftieth year, and I'm still on my quest to find a quiet mind. I begin to think that if I move out of the suburbs to the countryside, maybe the green energy of the bush will soften my sharp edges and quiet the noise.

This urge coincides with the end of Rowan's schooling. For fourteen years we've lived together, just the two of us, and now we're restless and want to discover new ways of being. Rowan's been awarded a University of Melbourne scholarship and wants to live in a share house, so we decide that she'll stay at our place and share it with her friends, and I'll take off to the bush.

On the first day I go looking, I find the house that I want to live in. It's on a hill at the edge of Warburton in the Yarra Ranges, surrounded by the foliage of mountain ash, beech and tree ferns. In just a few weeks, Pippa and I have moved out there and made it home. Pippa is protective, sharp as a whip, and she's been a constant companion to Rowan and me for twelve years.

Within a month of moving to Warburton, I learn that Pippa has cancer and is dying. Her sad brown eyes know it, and her body is weak. At night I lie with her on the floor in front of the fire, communing in the way that you can with a dog. During the day she likes to be carried to the car for a trip down to the river, where she lies on the grass in the sun watching the ducks, lifting her head slightly to sniff the air as they waddle past.

On a day when Mum and Irene are visiting from Canberra, Pippa can't stand up and her breathing is laboured. I ring the vet, who comes and gives her a lethal injection. She dies in Mum's arms. Irene digs a grave, and we bury her wrapped in a blanket. I always thought I'd be living in the bush here with Pippa. Her death teaches me something about mourning and, though I miss her, her loving energy remains in the house for weeks.

After Pippa's death, I lie in bed at night listening to frog songs, the mating sounds of wombats, the wind in the trees and the silence. I open myself to the energy of the place, write poetry and short stories, and sink into a kind of peace I've not experienced for a long time.

But after some months, that peace becomes stagnation. I am lost again. I find the starry beauty of the night cold and lonely, as if the abyss has swallowed me. I lose myself in the darkness of space, in a feeling of non-existence. I am nothing. As I walk along the banks of the Yarra through tree ferns and mountain ash, I try to convince myself that everything will be alright if I can just keep putting one foot in front of the other. If only I can just keep walking, endlessly moving through the landscape of trees and light. If only I can just keep walking, I'll be healed.

Around this time, my mother is diagnosed with Alzheimer's disease. She's no longer able to live on her own, so Irene moves to Canberra to live with her, and my brother Phil often drops in to visit. I ring Mum every second night, and we talk of family and everyday life. The bond between us deepens; life has given us a language we can share.

Rowan's birth brought a breakthrough and renewal in my relationship with both my parents. In motherhood my defensiveness melted; I could appreciate how much they must have suffered as a result of my madness, and how unbending I was with them. The highs and challenges of parenting have provided a common focus for Mum and me, while Dad's enthusiasm for all sorts of projects, from working for Saint Vincent de Paul to learning about computers, brought the two of us together. When he died five years ago, my mourning was helped by the rituals that Catholics do so well. I kissed his cold forehead as he lay in his coffin in the funeral house, and my grief broke open when 'Pie Jesu' was played at his Requiem Mass the next day. Now, years later, as Mum's memory falters and I sink into depression, we're a mutual support for each other through our phone calls and my visits to Canberra.

Whenever I walk along the riverbank at Warburton, a soft green energy bathes my mind. The Yarra is fresh and young up here in the mountains, and it rushes and tumbles over rocks in a torrent, home to platypus and fish, and a source of a vigorous energy. The vegetation is lush and varied, the mountain ash are tall and regal, and, in the night, the sky has more stars than I ever dreamed.

Even so, I can't escape the pain of my existence. I want to die. There's no obvious reason for this, but I can't stop thinking about dying. I draw deeply on Viktor Frankl's writings in order to shift this thought and develop strategies to get myself through the days. I know why I need to live; I just have to work out how.

I join the local library and begin a reading affair with memoirs written by solo sailors who circumnavigated the world in their small yachts. There are a huge number of these books, and I understand why – I can't get enough of them. There's something in their stories of solitary endurance that obsesses me. From their experiences of wild storms as they navigate the Horn and the Cape of Good Hope to their frustration at being becalmed in the Doldrums, I accompany them on their journeys. In their stories, I find the determination to get through each day as best I can, whatever the conditions in my inner world. Suffering is part of the deal. Endurance is all.

***

After two years at Warburton, I return to the city. I know that I need professional help again, but I don't know where to turn. Eventually I'm referred to a psychiatrist, and I feel that this is my last option. I tried medication before, and it didn't work for me, but I'll try it again because I'm desperate.

Fortunately for me, the psychiatrist's manner and methods of treatment are nothing like my experiences in the late 1960s and early '70s. This man has kind eyes, and he asks me questions about my inner world. He listens to my story, and we experiment with different antipsychotics, but they have powerful negative side effects; the mental relief that comes is undermined by heavy sedation, jangling nerves, mental fog and weight gain.

Then, after a couple of years during which I begin to think I'd prefer my madness to the side effects, the psychiatrist and I decide to try a new drug for schizophrenia that has recently become available.

What follows is remarkable. The side effects are minimal, and the madness retreats. A truce is declared; if I'm not stressed out, the noise remains behind enemy lines. I lose my fixation on death, and depression lets go of me. I'm aware of being sedated, and there's weight gain, but these are prices that I decide to pay for the relief I'm experiencing. I still have problems sleeping, but as long as I avoid situations that increase my anxiety, my mind is benign, considerate.

I'm now free to delight in ordinary, everyday things. This morning when I went out to collect the newspaper from my front garden, I breathed in the early morning air saturated with the smell of jasmine, lavender and earth, and it was like inhaling an elixir. I'm committed to an ongoing apprenticeship, learning how to live with the world as it is, with the self that I am. The world has let me come inside after all, and there are times when existence is quietly ecstatic. A singing, breathing life.

Julianne and Michael are on the inside of my soul, on the underside of my skin. They're alive as themselves in my inner world. I dream of them. I miss them. I keep having impressions of their presence – in the corner of a room, on a stairway or sitting across the table from me. For brief moments the other world forgets about me, and I'm cut loose to be with them again. In the darkness, in odd corners, they gather around me, the beloved dead, the original guardian angels. Sometimes they simply walk by me and are gone the instant I see them. Gone. Not gone. Gone.

I venture out on a new quest to explore the world around me. This time my quest-ion is: What will I do with this new life I've been given?

EPILOGUE

A Place in the World

In Scotland, as I walk the West Highland Way, my mind opens to the deep silence of the landscape, and my heart opens to sound: the wind, the rushing of a stream, my footsteps. Silence and sound, living within each other. There is no noise here – or in my mind.

I'm on the first of a series of walks I've planned for my five-month journey around Europe. I want to get to know the landscapes of countries that fire my imagination, and stay in cities I've always wanted to visit: Paris, Dublin, Barcelona, Prague. I have my pack and my maps, and I'm on my way.

On the first morning of my walk in Scotland, I leave the village of Tyndrum and pass through *Auch-ach innis chalean* (the field of the hazel meadow). The conical shape of Beinn Dorain appears before me, rising into blue sky. The weather is fresh and clear. Sunlight sparkles on the dew dotting the grasses along the track, and, on the mountain flanks, long drifts of purple heather disappear into the distance. Swallows and other small birds flit across the sky, and alders, birch and conifers cluster along the banks of streams and at the edge of a small loch.

As I walk beneath Beinn Dorain, I begin to feel its depth as my own depth, its reaching for the sky as my own reaching spirit. I'm soaring in this high, spare landscape, like the spellbound horses of the Dylan Thomas poem, walking out onto 'fields of praise'.

The next day I walk around the head of Loch Tulla, and then onto the vast expanse of Rannoch Moor. I pass hollows of scrubby myrtle and stop to rub the leaves together for the pleasure of inhaling their sweet perfume. Although a pale sun is shining, I'm alert to the weather; I've been warned that the moor is the most serious stretch of the West Highland Way because its exposed track offers no shelter and no easy retreat if the weather turns nasty.

The moor is wild and high. I'm alone with kestrels and falcons, wild heather, and the wind. I pass only one other walker as I make my way across this wide stretch of land. He raises his hand in a salute and continues on without slowing. The silence here is infinite. The space eternal. I feel as if I've dissolved, become elemental, at one with sky and distance.

Towards the end of the path across the moor, I find myself in the realm of the massive mountains of Coire Ba: Stob Dearg, Buachaille Etive Mor, Glen Etive and Glen Coe. They rise up like great songs do, disappearing into the immense silence of sky. I see a golden eagle, wings outstretched, gliding high. I take off my pack and sit on the ground, watching this flawless bird until it disappears behind a cloud. I find my bag of nuts and raisins, and take time to savour their sweetness and the fresh mineral taste of the water from my bottle. The mountains pound in my heart like drums.

Walking up a rise in the track across the moor, I see in the distance a white speck that must be the Kings House Hotel at Glencoe. I anticipate the sensation of drinking Guinness – the pleasure of quenching my thirst, and the smooth and bitter taste as the cool liquid slides down my throat. At the end of the day, I finally reach the hotel. The first thing I do is release the straps of my pack and let it sink to the ground. Then I make my way to the bar. Quietly euphoric, I buy a pint of Guinness.

The hotel's interior is dim, but I sense the mountains and their light all around me. I'm sore and tired, I need to have a shower and get out of these boots, but this Guinness fills me like a meal. As I sit at a table, after-images from my day's walk drift through my mind – heather and grasses, light on the surface of the lochs, mountain peaks. Little birds flitting and dipping in the air; the golden eagle that made me think of Michael. And I think with anticipation of the food I'm about to eat and the soft bed waiting for me. Bliss. Tomorrow I face the Devil's Staircase, and then my journey will continue down to Kinlochleven and on to Fort William.

***

After trekking along the West Highland Way, I go to Spain and walk part of the Camino de Santiago de Compostela, and later I walk around the wild west coast of Ireland. In between, I travel to Copenhagen, Prague, Wales and the Lake District of England.

I also go to Paris, in memory of Julianne and the trip that we never took. As I walk along a narrow Left Bank street, my thoughts are interrupted by the sense of her presence. She's walking with me, gesturing with her hands as she talks, her French self free and at home. The Seine flows like silky caramel between stone walls, street artists exhibit their paintings, and green sunlight shines in the trees along the riverbank.

Jules is here with me. In some reality, in some way, she is here. We've made it to Paris after all.

***

For the last leg of this five-month journey, Rowan and I meet up in Florence with plans to travel in Italy, Croatia and Turkey. We're both open to whatever comes our way, and we find each other easy company. We spend our days walking arm in arm through the winding streets of old European villages and sipping coffee in street cafes. We narrowly escape bed bugs in a hostel in Florence and share a single bed in the last budget hotel room available in Siena.

On the night crossing to Split in Croatia, we stand on the bow of the ferry sharing a small bottle of duty-free apricot brandy, exhilarated by the starry darkness, drunk on the pleasure of sea, wind and motion.

In Dubrovnik, we wander along the cobbled lanes of the old town and, at the end of the day, find a makeshift outdoor bar on a clifftop. Sitting in the warm evening, I become nostalgic as love songs from the 1950s play through the speakers and the blazing orb of the sun melts into the sea.

In Istanbul, we stand awestruck below the golden mosaics in the Aya Sophia. Later, with the wind in our hair, we ride a ferry down the Bosphorus to a small fishing village.

Throughout this journey, there are experiences of art, music, people, churches and, of course, food. I'm in love with the human imagination and spirit, and with that alchemical vessel, time. New thoughts appear, and I savour the enigmatic smells and the rush that comes with the illusion that I'm a stranger to myself, as if something of our exotic surroundings has rubbed off on me and I don't recognise who I am. Each new day is a festival, a ceremony of becoming, a rite of passage.

On the plane leaving Australia for this long journey, I wrote a poem that repeated the line, 'Everything that has happened before now is past.' Now, as I travel home, I grasp the truth of this thought. My madness has retreated, and I have confidence in the life opening up for me. This journey has been my pilgrimage to give thanks for the world that's welcoming me like a mother. More often than not, I can trust my mind to be steady and benign, and I've rediscovered the 'recreational thinking' that Julianne and I so enjoyed. I've also embarked on a wild, audacious love affair; it doesn't survive the distance between our home countries, but the memory remains, and the happiness.

As the plane comes in to land in Melbourne, I decide that I will go back to university and study Michael's poetry.

***

Life is very different for me now. While studying, I work part-time in a range of different jobs, including teaching young adults with intellectual disabilities and teaching English to carers in an aged-care facility. In 2006, I'm offered a part-time job at a university as a language and learning advisor. While doing this work, I complete a PhD. This study is life-changing and deeply rewarding, alongside my work with students and my colleagues – especially my colleagues. I'm one of the lucky ones: my workplace nourishes my soul as well as my material existence. I become grounded in the world. I sleep, really sleep, for the first time since Julianne died.

During these years, my relationship with Rowan grows and develops. In spite of the challenges she faced as a child and teenager, she's become a person whose nature is to love and create. She has a courageous intellect and has made a life for herself and a community of friends. She embraces what the world has to offer, explores ideas, and is curious and open. I'm immensely grateful to have Rowan in my life. She wants for me to be myself, despite everything, and this is what I want for her too – because of everything. Our relationship is a celebration of the life we live, sharing our thoughts and dreams, and the mundane burdens of our days.

As Michael wrote in a poem he gave me: 'The most of love is simply sharing.'

***

At the same time as I'm finding a place in the world, my mother is losing hers. As her Alzheimer's disease progresses and her memory fades, she loses herself, her family, her past. Every morning she looks blankly at Irene: 'Who am I?' she asks. 'Who are you?'

My sister gives her a few facts, some vivid paint strokes, an outline of a person: 'I'm your daughter, Irene. You're Pat Keogh. You were married to Ron for fifty-three years.'

'Did he love me?' Mum asks.

This is the question that, for more than a year, has been her obsession. At the end of her life, my mother wants to know if she was loved. She moves slowly into the day, feeling her way into her clothes, into the identity Irene constantly creates for her.

Sometimes Mum weeps quietly: 'I don't know where I am,' she says. Sometimes she's in extreme distress: 'Who am I?' she cries out from the doorway into her bedroom. Leaning on her walking frame, she pulls herself down the hall of the house where she's lived for over thirty years. 'Why am I here?' she asks of the space around her. Her mind is a watery bewilderness. Unborn thoughts float in her eyes. She takes tentative steps, one at a time.

My mother is a soul without a home, lost in the most absolute sense. There's no consolation in thinking that she doesn't know what's happening to her. Her suffering is her knowledge. She knows. She looked up at me the other day with eyes that had no light in them and asked me, 'Am I alive?' In the pause before I could answer, a hole opened in my heart. I took Mum's hand to comfort her, but she was unreachable, standing alone and lonely in some wild, inscrutable place on the very edge of life. I remembered the lines from Shakespeare's *King Lear:* 'As flies to wanton boys are we to th' gods,/They kill us for their sport.' And I thought to myself, *They do worse than that.*

Mum lingers in a lonely twilight, forgetting herself, her life, and those who love her. At the mid-point of the disease she still had language, the occasional spark of humour, the capacity for gratitude, and the ability to take pleasure in the sight of babies and the taste of ice-cream. But now, the loss of her self is devastating, totalising. Without memory you're lost in deep space.

When I was a child, the Russians sent a dog into orbit. I read about it in a newspaper that my father brought home from work. I remember standing at the table and staring at the photograph of a dog in a harness, sitting up in the spaceship. Her name was Laika. In response to my insistent questions, Dad admitted that there was no possibility of her returning to earth. When I was lying in bed at night, unable to sleep, I'd imagine Laika travelling alone through endless space, slowly starving to death. I pictured her sitting in the cockpit of the spacecraft, endlessly staring into the night sky. Totally alone. The only thread of consolation I could find was the hope that she didn't know what was happening to her. It was a slight hope, though. I believed she knew she'd be alone forever, strapped into the spaceship, dying of hunger and loneliness.

***

For fourteen years, Mum has been slowly fading away. Now, it's apparent that her life is coming to an end. I fly from Melbourne for a weekend with her in Canberra. Irene meets me at the airport and takes me to the nursing home where Mum has been for the past three weeks as her health has deteriorated. Irene tells us that she'll be back in the evening, and I take my place at Mum's bedside.

During these past weeks, Irene and Phil have been constantly by Mum's side, but Phil's away from Canberra this weekend. He made her laugh, and I always thought he was her favourite. Even after she didn't remember him, her face would light up when he visited, as if she knew that, whoever he was, he was someone she loved.

I spend the day with Mum, holding her hand and stroking her forehead. We sink into deep silences marked only by the sound of her breathing. At these times, as she fights for each breath, her stoic spirit fills the room. There's no doubt that she's engaged in a huge struggle, one harsh breath at a time. A nurse comes in and gives her morphine, then hands me a sheet of paper that lists the signs of impending death. I read it and put it to the side. I don't have any sense that Mum is going to die today.

I tell her stories of whatever comes to mind – her life, my life, our family – letting the narrative flow along its own course. Whenever something I say catches her attention, she looks at me and I'm held there, suspended in the open space of her gaze. I feel then as if we're floating together in the room, adrift, light as air. In between times, when my words fail and there's only the exertion of each rasping breath, I moisten her mouth with a small wet sponge and stroke her cool forehead.

As the day progresses, her skin takes on a bluish tinge, and she drifts in and out of awareness. I think of a brief exchange we had a couple of months before in a rare, lucid moment. 'Am I dying?' she asked, looking up at me from her chair as I bent down to take her plate. I could see, from her eyes, that there could be no evasion.

'Yes, Mum,' I said. 'I'm so sorry.'

'Is there any way to reverse the process?'

'No, I'm afraid there isn't. But you won't be on your own. Irene's here – we're all here with you.'

'Thank you,' she said, patting my hand.

In the evening, Irene and Annie arrive, and we gather around her. She seems to know that her three daughters are all here. On hearing of Mum's failing health, Annie immediately flew from East Timor to spend time with her. And Irene is standing by her, as she has for the past twelve years.

The night wears on, and Mum's struggle for each breath becomes more intense, a profound and stubborn fight for air. Then suddenly it changes, becomes lighter, a kind of wheezing. I realise she's dying. We hold her hands, smooth her forehead, talk to her softly. It's 11.15pm, and I tell her that it's nearly April Fools' Day, her wedding anniversary.

She looks at me with eyes that seem to be opening into the light, not closing off from it. An expanding, deepening consciousness. As if something vast is enfolding her. A full and pure emptiness. Then she breathes out and closes her eyes, and she doesn't breathe again. In that moment, a blade slices through my heart so smoothly, it feels like love.

***

While I've been writing this book, I've discovered that time is deep as well as long. I've read through my old notebooks and letters, relived experiences of love and madness, and danced again to the music I loved when I was young. I've also retraced my steps, returning to places that were important during the times I shared with Julianne and Michael.

I've walked the route that I used to take to Julianne's house, finding my way after all these years without having to think about it. I've also walked around the ANU campus, along the paths between the white poplars to Garran Hall where Julianne and I spent so much time in 1968. The trees are taller, the canopies thicker, there are new buildings among the older ones, but our younger selves still exist there somehow and have left an imprint, however subtle.

The places I associate with Michael haven't fared so well. Most of them have been destroyed or renovated beyond recognition. M Ward no longer exists. What had been the Canberra Hospital was demolished on 13 July 1997, in a staged event that was watched by over a hundred thousand people. One of these spectators, a twelve-year-old girl called Katie Bender, was killed when a fragment of the imploding building pierced her where she stood. A place that bore the histories of three or four generations of Canberra's population met its end in a tragic spectacle.

The National Museum of Australia now occupies the site on the peninsula where the hospital once sprawled. The area of lakeshore where Michael and I discovered the green bell was unrecognisable when I visited it in January 2010: the land surrounding the museum was parched by drought, and the few willows still growing along the bank were no longer lush and luxuriant. The green willow bell had disappeared.

In contrast, Lennox House just up the road from the museum has a happy ambience. Walls have been demolished in a renovation that's turned it into a community childcare centre. Small children play in colourful spaces that in the early '70s were run-down students' rooms, and workers' rooms in previous decades.

Other places have simply been superseded. The bungalow where Michael, Richard and Simon lived at Hall has been pulled down, and a new suburban house built on the block of land. And an ultra-modern hotel now stands in the place of the building that once housed Dimitri's restaurant.

Captains Flat is now home to a thriving if somewhat sleepy community. Empty houses have been renovated or carted away, the pub revitalised, and there's a cafe on the main street, frequented on weekends by daytrippers from Canberra. As part of a remediation program in the '70s, the slagheaps were covered in soil and planted with shrubs and other vegetation. Those old mounds of mine refuse have been recreated as small hills that blend into the surrounding countryside. The program has also reduced the toxic leachings into the river, and there's hope that native fish species will be re-established. Although it's taken a long time, the scars from the mine are healing.

Michael has gone, and lost also are the places that I associate with him. M Ward, the green bell, the bungalow at Hall and the slagheaps now exist only in memory. And in this story.

***

At odd moments I think of Michael and remember how it felt to be with him. I see now that a powerful drama was enacted in and through him during his short life. He interrogated male identity and sexuality, and he surrendered passionately to the psychological magnetism of myth and romanticism. In the crucible of his imagination and in his poetry, Michael constellated multiple identities. Ultimately, their competing visions and restless demands overwhelmed him. His death – and his identities – demonstrate the impossibility of someone with his complex psychological make-up leading a conventional life. He didn't conform to society's expectations of how a young male should live or who he should be.

Instead, Michael became a trickster, disobeying society's rules and challenging conventional codes of behaviour. A boundary-crosser, wise and foolish and boastful of his exploits, he used his poetic talent to cross between the real world and the realm of the imagination. There were times when, like an eagle, his spirit soared into the heights, 'above concrete and minimal existences, above idols and wars and caring'. Though he eventually became entangled in the depths, these experiences of soaring – and love – were his 'desiderata'.

He was a shapeshifter, a mischief-maker; now appearing in one form, now another. And he played at the periphery of the known, using his imagination to show us new worlds, drawing on his fantasies to reveal truths belonging to the other: the outsider, the exile, the freak. Michael was a brilliant poet, hypersensitive, kind and outrageous – and he bore the burden of his unique self gracefully and with courage.

Sometimes when I read the last lines of his poem 'Portrait of the artist as an old man', I wonder how it would be to pass an evening with Michael as an old man, sitting by a fire together, reflecting on life and on the times we shared. I wonder what he'd say, and what I would say. And if it would be as he described in his poem:

> *When night or winter comes, I light a fire*
> *and watch the flames*

rise and fall like waves. I regret nothing.

I can't say I have no regrets. There are a number of things that I would have done very differently – if I'd known how.

***

Until I wrote this memoir, the young woman I was in my early twenties was as distant from me as an actor in a film, even as I watched her enact my memories. Now, she's here within me, a second self, a wraith just under my skin. I see scenes and events as they emerge in memory through her eyes as well as my own. I feel her emotions, her pulse; I sense what she wanted. Both of us are here in the remembered moment. I'm with her as she moves her head to let her hair fall across her face like a curtain that she can hide behind. I feel in my body her breath and her instinctual life. I know the extremity of her desire and her dread. I've been there, inside her madness. And I'm tuned into her sensitivity to the energies of other people, to sounds and light and touch. I know her dreams.

I've discovered that she has always been with me, waiting to be born into language, waiting to speak and make sense of her life. She craved a face and two hands, and a mouth that could say true words. Now she has a face, lined with age but as much hers as it is mine. With both her hands, she held her newborn baby and nothing ever mattered more. And true words now rise up within her. She can speak. I can speak. She has given me back a part of myself that I thought I'd lost forever.

There are still times when people appear as unsolvable problems, and I continue to be challenged by social situations. If I allow myself to become stressed, my mind goes on the attack. But as Rilke says, 'What matters is to live everything.' There's no escape from the wounded state of the world or from our flawed humanity. I struggle with the obstinacy of primal emotions, with the daily claims of the real, and I grieve for the natural world. But I find that mostly I'm immersed in the moment, the people I love, the work I'm doing, the world I'm part of. Pain *and* joy, the middle way.

As I get older, the necessity of finding some meaning in the life I've lived becomes less urgent. Now, living life as a poem is more important than ever to me. I want to be present and aware in each moment, and eventually be awake to death when it comes. I hope to be conscious when I die, my heart and mind wide open.

In the meantime, the experiences I've had of love and loss help me live now, in these present moments. The enchantment and rapture of the green bell and the cold despair of the slagheaps remain as part of who I am. I love the moments of ecstasy that open me to the invisible world – but I also cherish the sensation of dwelling within the physical world and sharing ordinary human love and friendship, flawed and earthbound.

I know now that Michael was right, life *is* a poem, an encounter with the here and now of the imagined real. An excursion into its depths and reaches, its beauty and terror. And Julianne was right, the world is music playing. We live in this music, and it lives in us. The trick is tuning into it, listening for it. I have them both to thank for teaching me these truths. I'm grateful for everything, every moment we shared. I'm grateful, too, that the memory of our love and friendship endures and still moves me, still lives on in me. Sometimes it's the love that breaks through; other times it's the loss. And when they both emerge together, I find my old friends there, on the inside of my life.

A NOTE ON 1960s PSYCHIATRIC CARE

In 1960s Australia, it had only been a matter of years since the practice of lobotomising patients had fallen out of favour. For some time afterwards, treatments administered to people suffering from mental health problems continued to reflect a heavy-handed approach. Experimental methods were used with little accountability on the part of the doctors involved for deaths that occurred or adverse consequences of treatments.

One example of a tragic failure of the Australian psychiatric system during the 1960s and '70s occurred at the Chelmsford Private Hospital in Sydney. Between 1963 and 1979, twenty-four people died as a direct result of Deep Sleep Therapy (DST) administered at that hospital, and at least another twenty-two people committed suicide within twelve months of their treatment (New South Wales, Royal Commission into Deep Sleep Therapy, *Report* (1988), vol.4, 25, 37). DST is a procedure in which intravenous sedative and anti-psychotic drugs are given to patients to keep them in comatose or semi-comatose states for up to several weeks at a time (Royal Australian and New Zealand College of Psychiatrists, 'Position Statement 34: Deep Sleep Therapy,' 2009, http://www.ranzcp.org/Files/ranzcp-attachments/Resources/College_Statem

ents/Position_Statements/ps34-pdf.aspx (accessed December 21, 2012)). Doctors administer ECT while the patients are in the induced coma. DST was practised for seventeen years at the Chelmsford Private Hospital primarily by the psychiatrists Dr Harry Bailey and Dr John Herron, but other doctors were also involved (Ibid.).

The condition of patients undergoing this treatment should have been cause for alarm, if not urgent and immediate action. But over that whole period of time, no doctor involved in administering the therapy made a complaint. According to the *Report of the 1988 Royal Commission into Deep Sleep Therapy:*

> *large numbers of patients were treated for complications, these being mainly infections, pneumonia and deep vein thrombosis ... There was incontinence of urine and faeces and impaction and retention. There were restraints used to prevent falling from the bed, fractures and falls, vomiting, skin breakdown and metabolism imbalance. At the end of the treatment there were gross visual distortions and hallucinations and severe weakness. (New South Wales, Royal Commission into Deep Sleep Therapy, Report (1988), vol.4, 25, 37.)*

Only one medical professional, a nurse, made a complaint over a period of seventeen years. The nurse's complaint was made in 1970 to the Health and Public Service Board. It elicited a warning to Dr

Herron, but no other action was taken. There was no serious investigation until 1985, followed by the New South Wales Royal Commission into Deep Sleep Therapy (1988–1990).

As a result of its investigations, the Commission referred three doctors to the Director of Public Prosecutions. Dr Harry Bailey had committed suicide, but the other doctors fought the case in the High Court, which ultimately granted a permanent stay of disciplinary proceedings brought against them. In response to this ruling, the Director of Public Prosecutions dropped all charges (*Inside 60 Minutes: The Story Behind the Stories* (St Leonards, Sydney: Allen & Unwin, 1994), 42).

Julianne Gilroy did not die from DST. The connection is that her death occurred in Sydney at the same time that patients were dying at the Chelmsford Private Hospital in the same city. At this time (1963–1979), the circumstances surrounding conditions at Chelmsford suggest that a culture contaminated by hubris and incompetence developed unchecked within the psychiatric profession within New South Wales due to systemic failures within government and professional regulatory bodies.

Despite the inquiry into Julianne Gilroy's death, questions about her treatment and death have not been answered. It appears that no one was made accountable for her death. And the practices at the hospital where she died do not seem to have been subject to any official scrutiny.

REFERENCES

'The eyes are not here...' T.S. Eliot, 'The Hollow Men', *Collected Poems 1909–1962* (London: Faber & Faber, 1963), 91.

'doctor says how are you...' Paula Keogh, 'I swallow the pills', unpublished poem, September 1972.

'energy of ages...' Keogh, 'Where eyes would be', unpublished poem, September 1972.

I read a newspaper article ... 'S.M. finds girl died from drug poisoning', *The Sydney Morning Herald,* 8 April 1970, p.4.

'he is white pain...' Keogh, 'laugh at the sky', unpublished poem, September 1972.

'all is new...' Michael Dransfield, 'Always a season', *The Canberra Times,* 18 Nov 1972.

'prisoners of the Hotel Grand' Dransfield, 'paul and cathy,' *Collected Poems,* edited by Rodney Hall (St Lucia: University of Queensland Press, 1987), 361.

'Sorcerer, note how the stars...' Keogh, 'Michael', unpublished poem, October 1975.

'poetry is the blood in my veins...' Dransfield, 'Journal d'un Homme Vide', Diary March–April 1967, 23 March 1967, Papers of Michael Dransfield, MS 4741, National Library of Australia (hereafter cited as Dransfield MSS).

'and all his words...' Dransfield, 'Esais', *Collected Poems,* 43.

'the inspector of tides ... dressed in clouds...' Dransfield, 'The Inspector of Tides', *Collected Poems,* 116.

'haysheds and corners...' Dransfield, 'Minstrel', *Collected Poems,* 42.

'archaic ... rise and fall...' Dransfield, 'Portrait of the artist as an old man', *Collected Poems,* 17.

'the hermit ... imperfect silence ... it is enough', Dransfield, 'The hermit of green light', *Collected Poems,* 88.

'dreams of a perfect poem...' Dransfield, 'Miss Havisham', *Collected Poems,* 83.

'I am Proust...' Dransfield, 'Chaconne for a solipsist', *Collected Poems,* 243.

'love/let live ... Writ in the House of Torment...' Dransfield, 'The nature of passion', *Collected Poems,* 342

'The article appeared' ... Maurice Dunlevy, 'Poet who lives in the underground', *The Canberra Times,* 30 September 1972.

'Survival is the password...' Dransfield, Untitled poem, *Collected Poems,* 356.

'The ultimate commitment...' Dransfield, 'Like this for years', *Collected Poems,* 50.

'I cannot pull...' Dransfield, 'Still Life', *Collected Poems,* 356.

'statue and prayer/of the merciful...' Dransfield to Paula Keogh 1972.

'poisoning by an overdose...' Post-mortem report, Julianne Gilroy, 27 September 1968, quoted in Fraçoise Gilroy, née Droulers, *Mon Histoire: Memoirs of a French Australian* (Adelaide: Griffin Press, 2008), 189.

'In the beginning...' Bible, Genesis 1:1, King James Version.

'Words made flesh' Gospel according to John, 1.14, King James Version.

'I love you so intensely...' Dransfield to Paula Keogh, 24 October 1972, Dransfield MSS.

'How would you feel...' Ibid., 7 November 1972.

'We'll have a magic...' Ibid., 1 November 1972.

'you would get a good widow's pension...' Ibid., 7 November 1972.

'soul is worn out' Dransfield, 'Looking for somewhere kind', *Collected Poems,* 339.

'love/let live...' Dransfield, 'The nature of passion', *Collected Poems,* 342.

'o dearest sweet Paul' Dransfield to Paula Keogh, 31 October, Dransfield MSS.

'Got the shits real bad...' Ibid., 6 November 1972.

'You will meet her...' Ibid., 24 October 1972.

'midnight ... It's late...' Dransfield to Paula Keogh, 10 November 1972, Dransfield MSS.

'cleanse the doors of perception' This phrase is from William Blake's poem, 'The Marriage of Heaven and Hell' (1790), Plate 14: 'If the doors of perception were cleansed everything would appear to man as it is, infinite.' The metaphor is used by Aldous Huxley in his 1954 book, *The Doors of Perception,* in which he describes his experiences after taking the psychedelic drug, mescaline.

'displaced Romantics' Dransfield, 'No forwarding address', *Collected Poems,* 304.

'Drugs?...' Dransfield to Paula Keogh, 26 October 1972, Dransfield MSS.

'I've not had any...' Ibid., 1 November 1972.

'David is a poet...' The details of David Campbell's life in this paragraph come from *Australian Dictionary of Biography,* s.v. 'Campbell, David Watts (1915–1979)', http://adb.anu.edu.au/biography/campbell-david-watt-9680 (accessed December 5, 2012).

'Mirka describes herself as a "free spirit"...' Mirka Mora, interview by George Negus, *George Negus Tonight: Profiles,* ABC, 15 July 2004.

'Let us go hence...' This version of the poem is as Michael copied it from memory and gave me. The poem is Algernon Charles Swinburne's 'A Leave-Taking', from *The Poems of Algernon Charles Swinburne: In Six Volumes* (Cambridge: Chadwyck-Healey, 1992), ebook.

'only the wind and a river...' Dransfield, 'The hermit of green light', *Collected Poems,* 88.

'We die with the dying...' T.S. Eliot, 'Little Gidding, Four Quartets', *Collected Poems 1909–1962* (London: Faber and Faber Limited, 1963), 222.

'acute broncho-pneumonia and brain damage' 'The poet who kept on hating himself', *Sunday Mirror,* 7 October 1973, 25, quoted in Patricia Dobrez, *Michael Dransfield's Lives: A sixties biography* (Melbourne: Melbourne University Press, 1999), 509.

'we're much too close for any one...' Dransfield, 'Still life', *Collected Poems,* 355.

'I'm Prufrock...' T.S. Eliot, 'The Love Song of J. Alfred Prufrock', *Collected Poems 1909–1962* (London: Faber & Faber, 1963), 13.

'If only we would let ourselves...' Rainer Maria Rilke, 'The Man Watching', *Selected Poems of Rainer Maria Rilke,* translated by Robert Bly (New York: Harper & Row, 1981), 105.

'survival is *the password'* Dransfield, Untitled poem, *Collected Poems,* 356. (My emphasis).

'To blown straw...' Francis Webb, 'Five Days Old', *Collected Poems of Francis Webb,* edited by Toby Davidson (Crawley WA: UWAP, 2011), 225.

'If I may but touch...' Gospel according to Matthew 9:21, King James Version, 2000.

Martin Buber, *I and Thou,* edited by Walter Arnold Kaufmann (New York: Scribner, 1970).

Paul Tillich, *The Courage to Be* (New Haven: Yale University Press, 1952).

Viktor Emil Frankl, *Man's Search for Meaning: An Introduction to Logotherapy* (Boston: Beacon Press, 1992).

'fields of praise' Dylan Thomas, 'Fern Hill', from Jahan Ramazain, Richard Ellmann and Robert O'Clair (eds), *The Norton Anthology of Modern and Contemporary Poetry, Volume II* (New York: W.W. Norton & Company, 2003), 108.

'The most of love...' Dransfield to Paula Keogh, 1972.

'above concrete and minimal existences...' Dransfield, 'Geography III', *Collected Poems,* 66.

'When night or winter comes...' Dransfield, 'Portrait of the artist as an old man', *Collected Poems,* 17.

'What matters is to live everything' Rainer Maria Rilke, *Letters to a Young Poet & The Letter from the Young Worker,* edited and translated by Charlie Louth (London: Penguin, 2011), 23.

ACKNOWLEDGEMENTS

This book has its own life, one that began in my kitchen with conversations over a cup of tea or glass of wine with my daughter, Rowan Mangan. She became my travelling companion on this voyage back into my past and into the unknown of writing and memory. From the beginning, and despite my reticence, she believed this was a story that should be told. Her unswerving confidence in my ability to tell it spurred me on. Drawing on her brilliant writing skills and her profound understanding of the issues I was facing, she supported me through each phase of this journey. Her insights encouraged me to go deeper and further – and to keep going.

At the heart of this book are my dearest friends, Julianne Gilroy and Michael Dransfield. As I was writing and remembering, they became increasingly present in my inner world, giving of themselves almost as open-heartedly as they had when they were alive. Without them, this story would not exist; they are its heart, its rhythm and pulse. That Michael's voice can be heard in these pages is due to the kindness and generosity of his mother, Elspeth Dransfield. Her permission to quote from Michael's poems and letters allowed a vital thread and texture to be included in this story. Elspeth's gift and Michael's poem 'Geography III' have become for me the soul of the book.

Julianne came from a large and loving family whose warm encouragement and sensitive readings gave me firm ground beneath my feet. To Julianne's family, particularly her mother, Françoise Gilroy, and her sisters Andrée Ernest, Michelle O'Regan, and Yvette Gilroy, is owed this book's spirit – especially its commitment to celebrating Julianne's love of life and her passionate intellect.

There have been a number of heroes in the life of this book. Annie Keogh's readings, her wisdom and advice, and her deep understanding of the ethical and personal issues involved, have been a touchstone in my attempt to reach through to the emotional truth of the story.

With Rodney Hall, Michael's mentor, editor and friend, I exchanged memories and shared experiences of Michael's unique way of being in the world. These conversations and Rodney's generous reading of the manuscript made me realise that one of the things I wanted to do in these pages was capture Michael's mercurial spirit – despite knowing that such an aim was ultimately impossible.

As I attempted to open up to the real of the past, the insights of Patricia and Livio Dobrez, their thoughtful responses to the manuscript and their perceptive intuitions throughout the writing of the book, encouraged me to believe in the value of my subjective experience.

Other heroes of this book's life include Barbara Hiller, whose friendship, insights and sense of humour have been an inspiration and joy; Pat Walsh, Mayra Walsh, Joy Dahl, Sean Mangan, Annalea Beattie, Harry Zable and Penny Wagstaff for their invaluable readings and support; Diana Sima for kindly sharing her copies of photos; Christopher Ash for giving permission to use his photo for the cover and Garry Benson and Ros Osborne for their photos; and Kate McNamara for designating me 'the narrator of our youth', a blessing that was for me a moving and significant closing moment in this book's evolution.

I didn't start out with the intention of writing a memoir. Rather, I intended to write about Michael's poetry. The idea for the book came from Susan Bradley Smith, inspiring supervisor of my PhD thesis, and was supported by the staff in the English Department at La Trobe University.

My family, including my parents Ron and Pat Keogh, have been pivotal to this book's trajectory. They have given freely of their love and support throughout my life. My siblings' generous and personal responses to the manuscript reminded me that in every family there are hundreds of different stories. The enthusiastic support of mine, from Jane Irene Keogh, John Keogh, Jim Keogh, Anne Keogh, Phillip Keogh and Robert Keogh, propelled my memoir forward.

Finally, Martin Hughes and the great team at Affirm Press put their faith in this book, initially through their inaugural 2015 Mentorship Award and later through their work preparing it for publication. Kate Goldsworthy's committed and skilful editing has been vital; she has been midwife to its birth, expertly and gracefully ensuring its safe and healthy delivery into the world. Ruby Ashby-Orr has also given her editing expertise and insightful feedback. Varuna, the National Writers House, ran the Affirm Press Mentorship Program and provided an invaluable week-long residency in the beautiful Blue Mountains.

To all the above, I am deeply grateful. Without you, I wouldn't have completed this journey into the past or experienced the healing that telling my story made possible. Without your generosity and insights, this book would not be as it is or where it is. My heartfelt thanks.

My parents' marriage was a joyous occasion and a welcome break from the war. Their marriage was a love match but based on strict gender roles. My aspirations for my own marriage were to disrupt such roles, and to build an equal partnership.

At St Mary's Primary School, Braddon in 1959. My imagination was filled with stories of miracles and religious myths, and the dramatic lives and deaths of saints and martyrs. No wonder I was often in trouble for daydreaming, but it was hardly my fault!

In 1961, the Keogh family was living the '50s dream of the good life. A time of billycarts, barbecues along the Murrumbidgee, the nightly rosary and Sunday Mass. We were exuberant – and very innocent.

Julianne, my best friend from high school, whose death in 1968 led to my first two breakdowns. She was the one person who really knew me. After she died, I felt on the outside of life.

I didn't know that this photo was being taken, but I'm so pleased that it was: it perfectly captures the feelings I remember, being with Michael on the banks of the Murrumbidgee during a picnic with our dear friends. Christopher Ash took the photo.

Michael and me with our friend Simon Clough (second from the left), decked out in our hippy finery, chatting with another guest after our friend Chris Ash's wedding. My dress was made from curtain material, and Michael's waistcoat and beanie were from Nepal.

Love is in the air ... Chris embraces Michael and me at his wedding.

On a lazy day, hanging out together somewhere along the Murrumbidgee. Chris had set up his camera on the timer for a group shot – but his dog Issa got in the way as he tried to make it into the line-up.

When my good friend Garry Benson decided to take some photos in the front yard at Mann Terrace, I was wearing my favourite op-shop hat. A week later, I just missed being killed in a car accident and life turned upside-down again – but this time in a delightful way.

My daughter Rowan was a ragamuffin kid, cheeky and smart. She loved to make pies in the kindergarten sandpit, telling herself endless stories while she worked on her projects. Daydreaming runs in the family.

Rowan's joy is contagious, and Garry Benson captured her bright spirit in this photo of us.

On my overseas odyssey. I had just walked the Devil's Staircase, one of the steepest sections of the West Highland Way in Scotland. Next time I'll make sure my pack is lighter!

The sun was setting, the moon rising. At the magical winter solstice, Rowan and I were alone on the Hill of Tara, Ireland. The evening was enchanted, and we were ecstatic - and my nose red from the freezing cold.

My mother, Pat Keogh, with one of her favourite paintings. She treasured a poem about gum trees that Michael wrote for her. They weren't just trees to her: they were her spirit emblem.

This was the last time the Keogh siblings gathered at the family home in Hackett: Jim, Robert, Phil and John (from left, back), and Paula, Irene and Annie (from left, front). We reminisced and drank toasts to our parents.

On the day of my PhD graduation, I was feeling quite philosophical. Still couldn't quite believe I'd actually finished my thesis. I relished the chance to study issues related to mental health, and to try to make sense of a clamorous time in my life.

Back Cover Material

'A courageous account of madness. Paula Keogh has brilliantly captured its creative exhilaration, illumination, grief and loss. She takes us on a deeply human search for integrity and meaning.'

Kate Richards, author of *Madness: a memoir*

In 1972, Paula Keogh and Michael Dransfield meet in the psychiatric ward of the Canberra Hospital and instantly fall in love. Michael is being treated for a drug addiction; Paula is delusional and grief-stricken.

Paula recovers a self that she thought was lost, while Michael, a radical poet, is inspired to write the poems that become *The Second Month of Spring.* Together, they plan for 'a wedding, marriage, kids – the whole trip'. But outside the hospital, madness and grief challenge their luminous dream. Can their love survive?

The Green Bell is a lyrical and profoundly moving memoir about love and madness. Ultimately, it reveals itself to be a hymn to life. A requiem for lost friends. A coming of age story that takes a lifetime.

'In 1972, Paula Keogh fell in love with Michael Dransfield, the most gifted poet of his generation. Her portrait of him – and the brief period they spent

together – recaptures that time with remarkable freshness and insight.'

Rodney Hallr

Made in United States
Orlando, FL
16 December 2025

74883823R00188